HOW TO BE AN EXPLORER OF THE WORLD

PORTABLE ~~ART~~ LIFE MUSEUM

KERI SMITH

PENGUIN BOOKS

PENGUIN BOOKS

AN IMPRINT OF PENGUIN RANDOM HOUSE LLC
375 HUDSON STREET
NEW YORK, NEW YORK 10014
PENGUIN.COM

FIRST PUBLISHED IN THE UNITED STATES OF AMERICA BY PERIGEE, AN IMPRINT OF PENGUIN GROUP
(USA) INC., 2008
PUBLISHED IN PENGUIN BOOKS 2016

LIBRARY OF CONGRESS CATALOGING-IN-PUBLICATION DATA
SMITH, KERI.
HOW TO BE AN EXPLORER OF THE WORLD : PORTABLE LIFE MUSEUM / KERI SMITH.—1ST ED.
P.   CM.
ISBN 978-0-399-53460-7

PRINTED IN THE UNITED STATES OF AMERICA
28TH PRINTING

CONTENTS

HOW TO USE THIS BOOK...2

EXPLORATION #1: RIGHT WHERE YOU ARE SITTING...28

EXPLORATION #2: EXPERIENCE COLLECTION...30

EXPLORATION #3: LIGHT...32

EXPLORATION #4: DAILY WALK...34

EXPLORATION #5: THE FIRST THING YOU SEE...36

EXPLORATION #6: ARCHAEOLOGICAL DIG...40

EXPLORATION #7: WORLD OF COLOR...42

EXPLORATION #8: CRACKS...44

EXPLORATION #9: CASE OF CURIOSITIES...46

EXPLORATION #10: ONE THING...48

EXPLORATION #11: DIFFERENCES...50

EXPLORATION #12: FIFTY THINGS...52

EXPLORATION #13: COLLECTING TYPE...54

EXPLORATION #14: SOUND MAP...56

EXPLORATION #15: CONSUMER...58

EXPLORATION #16: SURVEY...60

EXPLORATION #17: INSTANT SCULPTURE...62

EXPLORATION #18: STRUCTURE...64

EXPLORATION #19: FOUND "PAINT"...66

EXPLORATION #20: SMALL THOUGHTS...68

EXPLORATION #21: YOUR FAVORITE STREET...70

EXPLORATION #22: PEOPLE WATCHING...72

EXPLORATION #23: HOW TO UNCOVER A MYSTERY...74

EXPLORATION #24: COMBINATIONS...76

EXPLORATION #25: WATER...78

EXPLORATION #26: BECOMING LEONARD COHEN...80

EXPLORATION #27: ACCIDENTAL ART...82

EXPLORATION #28: BLIND OBSERVATION...84

EXPLORATION #29: TACTILE BOARDS...86

EXPLORATION #30: TRAVEL HISTORY...88
EXPLORATION #31: FOUND SOUNDS...90
EXPLORATION #32: WORLD OF MAGIC...92
EXPLORATION #33: ARRANGEMENTS...94
EXPLORATION #34: INTERESTING GARBAGE...96
EXPLORATION #35: INVISIBLE CITY...98
EXPLORATION #36: THE TRUTH ABOUT INANIMATE OBJECTS...100
EXPLORATION #37: TIME OBSERVATION...102
EXPLORATION #38: GROCERY SHOPPING WITH JOHN CAGE...104
EXPLORATION #39: FOOD AS ART...106
EXPLORATION #40: ALTERED STATES...108
EXPLORATION #41: FOUND FACES...110
EXPLORATION #42: LOCAL LORE...112
EXPLORATION #43: FOUND PAPER...114
EXPLORATION #44: LIBRARY EXPLORATION...116
EXPLORATION #45: SELF-ETHNOGRAPHY...118
EXPLORATION #46: FOUND PATTERNS...120
EXPLORATION #47: THE SHAPES OF STAINS AND SPLOTCHES...122
EXPLORATION #48: FINDER EXPLORATION...124
EXPLORATION #49: FOUND WORDS...126
EXPLORATION #50: FOUND SMELLS...128
EXPLORATION #51: NON-LINEAR LIFE...130
EXPLORATION #52: MINIATURE ECOSYSTEM...134
EXPLORATION #53: FOUND WRITING UTENSILS...136
EXPLORATION #54: THE LANGUAGE OF TREES...138
EXPLORATION #55: WAYS TO TRANSFORM AN EVERYDAY EXPERIENCE...140
EXPLORATION #56: HOW TO INCORPORATE INDETERMINACY...142
EXPLORATION #57: THOUGHT EXPERIMENTS...144
EXPLORATION #58: SCAVENGER HUNT COLLECTION...146
EXPLORATION #59: HOW TO WANDER AIMLESSLY...148
FIELD WORK...150
SETTING UP A SHOWING...192

GLOSSARY...198
BIBLIOGRAPHY...200
THANK-YOUS...204

EHI PASSIKO*

*AN INVITATION TO "COME AND SEE" IN THE ANCIENT PALI LANGUAGE.

WE SHALL NOT CEASE FROM EXPLORATION

AND THE END OF ALL OUR EXPLORING

WILL BE TO ARRIVE WHERE WE
                    STARTED

AND KNOW THE PLACE FOR THE
                FIRST TIME.

—T.S. ELIOT, "THE FOUR QUARTETS"

HOW TO USE THIS BOOK

1. READ IN ANY ORDER.
   USE FIELDWORK SECTION IN THE
   BACK OF THE BOOK TO RECORD
   AND DOCUMENT FINDINGS.

2. ALL EXERCISES ARE OPEN TO
   INTERPRETATION.

3. FEEL FREE TO ADD, ALTER, OR IGNORE.

4. THERE ARE NO RULES, MERELY
   SUGGESTIONS.

5. TREAT EVERYTHING AS AN
   EXPERIMENT.

6. START WITH WHATEVER MAKES
   YOU FEEL A TWINGE OF EXCITEMENT.

OFTEN INTERESTING THINGS CAN BE HIDDEN IN THE CRACKS. ⟶

AUTHOR'S NOTE: NONE OF THE IDEAS IN THIS BOOK ARE NEW. MANY OF THEM HAVE BEEN PILFERED, BORROWED, ALTERED, AND STOLEN FROM GREAT THINKERS AND ARTISTS OF OUR TIME. I HAVE MADE AN ATTEMPT TO CITE ALL ROOT SOURCES (THOSE THAT ARE KNOWN TO ME) OF THESE IDEAS IN THE BIBLIOGRAPHY, AS WELL AS ADDING CITATIONS IN EACH SECTION TO LEAD YOU TO FURTHER READING ON A GIVEN SUBJECT. A LOT OF THE INFORMATION IN THIS BOOK WAS ACQUIRED BY READING THESE BOOKS. BUT THE REAL LEARNING OF THESE METHODS IS TO BE HAD (IN THE WORDS OF ANAÏS NIN) "IN THE MIDST OF LIVING."

THIS BOOK STARTED WITH A LIST
THAT I WROTE ONE NIGHT WHEN
I COULDN'T SLEEP...

THESE IDEAS ARE AN ACCUMULATION
OF THINGS THAT I HAVE LEARNED FROM
VARIOUS TEACHERS AND ARTISTS OVER
THE YEARS AND HAVE BECOME THE
BASIS FOR ALL OF MY OWN EXPLORATION.
THEY ALL SPEWED OUT AT ONCE...

HOW TO BE AN EXPLORER OF THE WORLD

1. ALWAYS BE LOOKING.

   (NOTICE THE GROUND BENEATH YOUR FEET.)

2. CONSIDER EVERYTHING ALIVE & ANIMATE.

3. EVERY THING IS INTERESTING. LOOK CLOSER.

4. ALTER YOUR COURSE OFTEN.

5. OBSERVE FOR LONG DURATIONS (AND SHORT ONES).

6. NOTICE THE STORIES GOING ON AROUND YOU.

7. NOTICE PATTERNS. MAKE CONNECTIONS.

8. DOCUMENT YOUR FINDINGS (FIELD NOTES) IN A VARIETY OF WAYS.

9. INCORPORATE INDETERMINANCY.

10. OBSERVE MOVEMENT.

11. CREATE A PERSONAL (DIALOGUE) WITH YOUR ENVIRONMENT. TALK TO IT.

12. TRACE THINGS BACK TO THEIR ORIGINS.

13. USE ALL OF THE SENSES. IN YOUR INVESTIGATIONS.

AFTER READING THIS LIST A FEW TIMES IT OCCURRED TO ME THAT...

ARTISTS AND SCIENTISTS ANALYZE THE WORLD AROUND THEM IN SURPRISINGLY SIMILAR WAYS.

OBSERVE
COLLECT
ANALYZE
COMPARE
NOTICE
PATTERNS

7

WHEN I LOOK CLOSELY AT THE WORK OF ALL
MY FAVORITE ARTISTS AND DESIGNERS I NOTICE
THE ALL HAVE ONE THING IN COMMON...
THEY ARE <u>COLLECTORS</u>.

THIS TENDENCY TO COLLECT AND
DOCUMENT IS SIMILAR TO THE
WORK OF AN ETHNOGRAPHER.

ETHNOGRAPHY. N. THE DOCUMENTATION
AND ANALYSIS OF A PARTICULAR
CULTURE THROUGH FIELD RESEARCH.

EVERYTHING IS
INTERESTING

EVERYTHING HAS A VALUE, PROVIDED IT
APPEARS AT THE RIGHT PLACE AT
THE RIGHT TIME. IT'S A MATTER
OF RECOGNIZING THAT VALUE, THAT
QUALITY, AND THEN TO TRANSFORM IT
INTO SOMETHING THAT CAN BE USED.
IF YOU COME ACROSS SOMETHING
VALUABLE AND TUCK IT AWAY IN
YOUR METAPHORICAL SUITCASE THERE'S
SURE TO COME A MOMENT WHEN
YOU CAN MAKE USE OF IT.
— JURGEN BEY

9

WHICH BRINGS US TO...

YOUR MISSION

TOP SECRET

IF FOUND, DO
NOT OPEN.

(PROCEED WITH CURIOSITY.)

YOU ARE AN EXPLORER.

YOUR MISSION IS TO DOCUMENT AND OBSERVE THE WORLD AROUND YOU AS IF YOU'VE NEVER SEEN IT BEFORE. TAKE NOTES. COLLECT THINGS YOU FIND ON YOUR TRAVELS. DOCUMENT YOUR FINDINGS. NOTICE PATTERNS. COPY. TRACE. FOCUS ON ONE THING AT A TIME. RECORD WHAT YOU ARE DRAWN TO.

DO THIS WHEREVER YOU ARE (AT ANY TIME, AT THE GROCERY STORE, ON YOUR WAY TO WORK, WAITING IN LINE AT THE BANK, OR EVEN IF YOU ARE SICK IN BED). YOU DO NOT HAVE TO TRAVEL TO FARAWAY PLACES (THOUGH YOU MAY DECIDE TO DO THIS AT SOME POINT ON YOUR ADVENTURES). YOU DO NOT NEED LARGE AMOUNTS OF TIME.

YOU MIGHT WANT TO THINK OF THIS BOOK AS YOUR METAPHORICAL SUITCASE. A PLACE TO COLLECT AND DOCUMENT YOUR FINDINGS. HOW DO YOU SEE? IT IS ALSO A MUSEUM. YOUR VERY OWN MUSEUM THAT WILL CONTAIN YOUR UNIQUE VISION OF THE WORLD.

IT WILL BE DIFFERENT FROM ANY OTHER MUSEUM IN THE WORLD BECAUSE YOU ARE UNIQUE. YOU CAN ADD TO IT AT ANY TIME; YOU CAN TOUCH ALL OF THE THINGS IN IT. EVERYTHING IN IT IS FREE. BEST OF ALL, IT IS PORTABLE. PERFECT FOR TAKING WITH YOU ON YOUR TRAVELS. (YOU CAN HAVE SPONTANEOUS SHOWINGS WHEREVER YOU ARE.) SELL TICKETS (OR NOT). IT CHANGES AS YOUR PERCEPTION OF THE WORLD CHANGES. YOU CAN VISIT YOUR MUSEUM WHENEVER YOU NEED IDEAS (OR IF YOU WANT TO SEE WHAT IS FLOATING AROUND IN YOUR BRAIN).

IMPORTANT

READ ON ONLY IF YOU ACCEPT

YOUR MISSION.

THE FOLLOWING PAGES INCLUDE A
VARIETY OF PROMPTS AND ASSIGNMENTS
THAT WILL HELP YOU ON YOUR TRAVELS.
THERE IS ALSO A SECTION ON TOOLS
AND TECHNIQUES THAT WILL HELP YOU
WITH DOCUMENTING METHODS.
YOU MAY USE THE WORKSHEETS
INCLUDED OR CREATE YOUR OWN.
REMEMBER, ALL OF YOUR MOST
IMPORTANT TOOLS EXIST IN YOUR
BODY! USE THEM. COLLECT AS
MUCH DATA AS YOU CAN— IT MAY
COME IN HANDY LATER ON. GOOD
LUCK ON YOUR JOURNEY.

WHERE TO BEGIN (IN WHICH WE BECOME COMFORTABLE WITH LIVING THE QUESTIONS).

ON MY DESK I HAVE A LITTLE JAPANESE BOWL FILLED WITH SEA GLASS. I CAN SPEND HOURS TAKING THE PIECES OUT AND EXAMINING THEM. SORTING, ARRANGING, PUTTING THEM INTO GROUPS ACCORDING TO SIZE, SHAPE, THEN COLOR. HOLDING EACH ONE IN MY HAND AND FEELING THE SURFACES. EXAMINING THEM FOR THEIR UNIQUE QUALITIES, MARKS, CRACKS, HISTORIES. HOLDING THEM UP TO THE LIGHT, TRYING TO LOOK THROUGH THEM.

THIS ONE HAS A PLACE THAT FITS MY THUMB PERFECTLY. THIS ONE HAS THE SLIGHTEST TINT OF ROBIN'S-EGG BLUE. THIS ONE STILL HOLDS SOME OF THE SHAPE OF THE ORIGINAL BOTTLE IT CAME FROM. I PONDER HOW ALL THESE PIECES ENDED UP IN THE OCEAN. WHAT JOURNEY HAVE THEY BEEN ON? HOW MANY HANDS TOUCHED THEM BEFORE MINE? WHAT DIFFERENT KINDS OF SOUNDS CAN I MAKE WITH THEM? DO THEY HAVE A TASTE? THERE ARE THINGS I WILL NEVER KNOW ABOUT THEM. BUT THERE ARE ALSO THINGS I CAN UNCOVER. I DEVELOP MY OWN EXPERTISE AS I GO AND UNDERSTAND IT IS BASED ON MY PERSONAL OBSERVATIONS.

THERE IS NO "CORRECT" WAY OF UNDERSTANDING ANYTHING. (EVEN THOUGH THE WORLD WANTS US TO BELIEVE THIS, IT'S NOT TRUE.)

THE INDO-EUROPEAN ROOT OF THE WORD "ART" IS "TO ARRANGE" OR "FIT TOGETHER" (JOIN). IN THIS LIGHT, ART CAN BE PARED DOWN TO ITS MOST SIMPLISTIC FORM. <u>WE BEGIN BY COLLECTING</u>, THEN PLAYING WITH THE MATERIALS OR OBJECTS, ORGANIZING THEM IN A VARIETY OF WAYS, MAKING NEW COMBINATIONS, TRYING THINGS, THEN OBSERVING THE ARRANGEMENTS WE HAVE MADE.

16

COLLECT ITEMS YOU FANCY AND
THAT FOR DIFFERENT
REASONS ATTRACT YOUR
ATTENTION. REMEMBER ALSO
TO COLLECT AND STUDY THINGS
THAT SEEM FOR THE MOMENT TO
BE MEANINGLESS OR IRRELEVANT.
THE TWISTS AND TURNS OF
THE CREATIVE PROCESS LEAD
YOU BACK TO AN IMPORTANT
ENCOUNTER THAT AT FIRST SEEMED
QUITE NEUTRAL OR EVEN SOMETHING
THAT MADE YOU FEEL REPELLED
OR EXASPERATED.
— MAJA RATKJE

17

METHODS OF INVESTIGATION

OUR PERCEPTION OF THINGS CAN BE ALTERED SIMPLY BY THE ANGLE WE CHOOSE TO LOOK AT SOMETHING.

AN AVERAGE TREE LOOKS VERY DIFFERENT DEPENDING ON IF WE VIEW IT FROM FAR AWAY OR CLOSE UP. IT CHANGES AGAIN IF WE CHOOSE TO LOOK AT IT AS A COLOR PALETTE. MAYBE YOU DECIDE TO STUDY IT IN SEPERATE PARTS: THE LEAVES, THE BARK, THE GROWTH PATTERNS, THE ROOT SYSTEM. YOU COULD ALSO CHOOSE TO SEE HOW A TREE HAS FUNCTIONED IN A COMMUNITY (AS A MEETING PLACE), OR ANECDOTALLY—WHAT STORIES DO THE PEOPLE WHO LIVE AROUND IT HAVE TO TELL? WHO PLANTED IT? WHAT SOUNDS ARE MADE BY THE TREE? WHAT DOES THE SPACE AROUND THE TREE LOOK LIKE? WHAT IS IT MADE OF? HOW DOES THE TREE CHANGE VISUALLY OVER THE COURSE OF A DAY? A YEAR?

CREATIVITY ARISES FROM OUR ABILITY TO
SEE THINGS FROM MANY DIFFERENT ANGLES.

WAYS OF SEEING

THE FOLLOWING LIST INCLUDES A FEW OF THE
METHODS THAT WE CAN USE IN OUR INVESTIGATIONS.
WE CAN MAKE DECISIONS TO LOOK AT THINGS IN
A VARIETY OF WAYS AT ANY TIME. THIS IS
ONLY A PARTIAL LIST.   YOU CAN ADD TO
IT YOURSELF AS

YOU GO.

SIGHT, SOUND, SMELL, TOUCH, TASTE, MOVEMENT,
SHAPE, TEXTURE, FUNCTION, SYMBOL, LANGUAGE
(DEFINITION, WORDS), SUBJECTIVELY, OBJECTIVELY,
CONTRAST, NEGATIVE SPACE,
IN COMPARISON, COLOR, IN PARTS, ANECDOTALLY
SYMMETRICALLY, ARTISTICALLY, SCIENTIFICALLY,
(AS A STORY), HISTORICALLY, SYNCHRONICALLY
MORALLY, DIACHRONICALLY (ACROSS TIME), CONTEXTUALLY,
(ONE POINT IN TIME), METAPHYSICALLY,
CULTURALLY, POLITICALLY, RITUALISTICALLY, IN MULTIPLE,
AESTHETICALLY, MICRO, MACRO, ABSTRACTEDLY,
ALONE, 2D, 3D, DIRECTIONALLY,
MYTHICALLY, AS A HABITAT,
LINEARLY, AS A DEVICE,
LIGHTHEARTEDLY,
AS A
SIGN.

19

DOCUMENTING AND COLLECTING METHODS AND TOOLS

TO BE AN EXPLORER YOU DO NOT NEED ANY FANCY MATERIALS. ALL OF THE EXERCISES IN THIS BOOK CAN BE DONE USING WHATEVER YOU HAVE (JUST A PENCIL AND THIS BOOK). AS YOU GO ALONG YOU MAY WISH TO EXPLORE MORE DETAILED METHODS DEPENDING ON WHAT YOU HAVE AT YOUR DISPOSAL. HERE IS A SHORT LIST OF VARIOUS METHODS (YOU CAN ADD TO THIS LIST AS YOU DISCOVER NEW METHODS):

SIMPLE METHODS: WRITING, SKETCHING, COLLECTING OBJECTS, PENCIL RUBBINGS, PRESSINGS (FLAT OBJECTS), TRACING, CLAY RELIEF (PLASTICINE), TRANSCRIBING (CONVERSATIONS), PRINT MAKING (USING OBJECTS)

MORE INVOLVED TOOLS (OPTIONAL)

CAMERA/ PHOTOS

NON-DRYING MODELING CLAY (PLASTICINE)

TWEEZERS

GLUE

GLOVES

TAPE

SOME KIND OF BAG

AUDIO RECORDER, MP3 PLAYER, COMPUTER, ETC.

VIDEO CAMERA

MAGNIFYING GLASS

FIELDBOOK FOR TAKING NOTES

DATE STAMP & PAD

POCKET KNIFE

PENCIL & PENS

LABELS

METHODS OF COLLECTING

ZIPLOC BAGS

ENVELOPES

RECYCLED GLASS JARS

RECYCLED BOXES

JOURNAL

PILL JARS OR FILM CONTAINERS

FILE FOLDERS

ALTOIDS CANDY TINS

TACTILE BOARDS

HANGING

A LIST OF THINGS TO DOCUMENT AND COLLECT

YOUR COLLECTIONS AND RESEARCH SHOULD BE MADE UP OF THINGS THAT YOU RESPOND TO. THIS PROCESS IS BASED ON COLLECTING OR DOCUMENTING THINGS THAT EXIST FOR FREE IN THE ENVIRONMENT. THEY SHOULD BE THINGS THAT ARE READILY AVAILABLE OR FOUND, NOT PURCHASED. USE THIS LIST AS A LEAPING OFF POINT FOR INVESTIGATION.

THE CREATIVE MIND PLAYS WITH THE OBJECTS IT LOVES.
— CARL JUNG

OFFICE SUPPLIES
SIGNATURES
FEATHERS
WHISKERS
WORDS
OFF CUTS
THINGS FROM THE OCEAN
STRIPES
LEAVES
GRASSES
MAPS
REFLECTIONS
FOOD
THINGS THAT DECAY
FRUIT STICKERS
IDEAS
TYPE/LETTERING
OPPOSITES
FLAT THINGS
THINGS THAT MELT
COFFEE CUPS
THINGS THAT SURPRISE YOU
REFLECTIONS
MOSS
INTERESTING BEHAVIORS
ROUND THINGS
DEAD INSECTS
WISHES
TAPE
OVERHEARD CONVERSATIONS
STAINS
STICKY THINGS
CRACKS
SMELLS
CHARACTERS
SPICES
WAX
LINT
THREAD
LISTS
TEXTURES
MOLD
SHADOWS
STICKERS
SEMI CIRCLES
PAPER
GROWTH PATTERNS
SEED PODS
DIRT
THINGS FROM TREES
DETRITUS
AIR
WIRE
NUMBERS
STRING
DREAMS
FOUND FACES
LONG SKINNY THINGS
CLOUD SHAPES
KNOTS
THINGS THAT HANG
SHELLS
COCOONS
PACKAGING
SOUNDS
COLORS
JUNK MAIL
WATER
PEN LINES
RESIDUE
HOLES
SCRATCHES
FABRIC
WRINKLES
DUST
APOLOGIES
ABSURD THINGS
THINGS ON THE SIDEWALK
PLASTIC THINGS
GRIDS
FOUND PHOTOS
SHOE SOLES
STICKS
REALLY TINY THINGS
PENCIL RUBBINGS
IMPRESSIONS
QUESTIONS
SUGAR PACKAGES
STORIES
ARROWS
THINGS THAT LOOK LIKE OTHER THINGS
VESSELS
NESTS
SECURITY PATTERNS ON ENVELOPES
RUBBER BANDS
MANHOLE COVERS
THINGS IN THE SKY

23

LIFE IS A SCAVENGER HUNT

FIELDWORK TIPS

1. NEVER LEAVE HOME WITHOUT A NOTEBOOK AND PEN.

2. WHEN PRACTICING "DEEP LOOKING" OR "DEEP LISTENING" IT IS BEST TO WORK ALONE.

3. RESPECT THE COMMUNITY IN WHICH YOU EXPLORE. THIS APPLIES TO ASPECTS OF NATURE, HUMAN OR OTHERWISE (AND ALSO INCLUDES PROPERTY, PUBLIC OR PRIVATE).

4. IF YOU FIND YOURSELF BEING QUESTIONED AS TO THE REASONS FOR YOUR ACTIVITIES, THE PHRASE "I'M CONDUCTING RESEARCH" USUALLY SATISFIES THE NOSIEST INTERLOPER.

5. EXPECT THE UNEXPECTED (AND YOU WILL FIND IT).

ANYTHING CAN BE A STARTING PLACE.

BEGIN WHERE YOU ARE.

IS THAT TOO VAGUE? OKAY, THEN TURN THE PAGE.

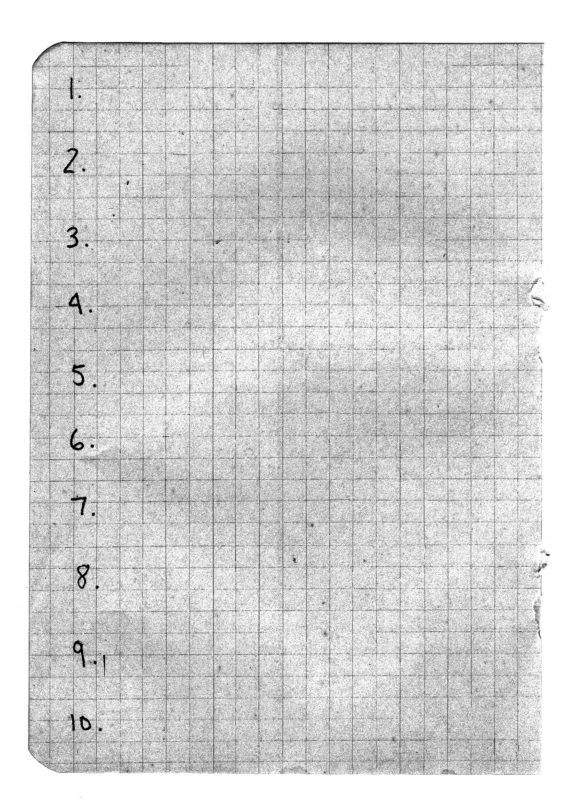

1.

2.

3.

4.

5.

6.

7.

8.

9.1

10.

28

RIGHT WHERE YOU ARE SITTING

WRITE TEN THINGS ABOUT WHERE YOU ARE SITTING RIGHT NOW THAT YOU HADN'T NOTICED WHEN YOU SAT DOWN. USE YOUR SENSES. DO IT QUICKLY. DO NOT CENSOR. OKAY, BEGIN.

THE ASPECTS OF THINGS THAT ARE MOST IMPORTANT FOR US ARE HIDDEN BECAUSE OF THEIR SIMPLICITY AND FAMILIARITY. (ONE IS UNABLE TO NOTICE SOMETHING-BECAUSE IT IS ALWAYS BEFORE ONE'S EYES.) —LUDWIG WITTGENSTEIN

DIRECTIONS

TAKE TWO WITH WATER
FOLLOWED BY A LONG
WALK.

RANDOM
EXPERIENCE
GENERATION
PILLS

EXPERIENCE COLLECTION

USING THE "EXPERIENCE LOGS" IN THE
BACK OF THE BOOK, MAKE A LIST
OF THINGS THAT YOU NOTICE ON YOUR
TRAVELS OR EXPERIENCES YOU HAVE.
THEY COULD BE VERY BRIEF NOTES
INCLUDING LOCATION, TIME, DATE, ETC.

EVERY EXPERIENCE IS UNREPEATABLE.
-ITALO CALVINO

LIGHT

COLLECT OBJECTS BASED ON
HOW THEY REFLECT LIGHT.
LIST THE DIFFERENT QUALITIES,
SUCH AS REFLECTIVE, TRANSLUCENT,
REFRACTING, MOTTLED, ETC. (TRY
TO COLLECT THIRTY OBJECTS.)

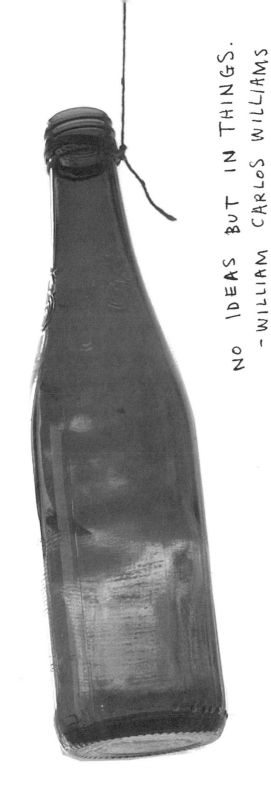

NO IDEAS BUT IN THINGS.
— WILLIAM CARLOS WILLIAMS

EXPLORATION #3

ALTERNATE: LIGHT VISION
START TO PAY ATTENTION TO
LIGHT PATTERNS, REFLECTIONS,
AND PROJECTIONS. CONSIDER
THAT THEY ARE EVERYWHERE.
DOCUMENT THEM.

*GLUE AN ENVELOPE OR PLASTIC BAGGY HERE.

EVERY MORNING WHEN WE WAKE UP, WE HAVE TWENTY-FOUR BRAND-NEW HOURS TO LIVE. WHAT A PRECIOUS GIFT!
—THICH NHAT HANH

DAILY WALK

COLLECT OBJECTS ONLY ON YOUR
WAY TO WORK OR SCHOOL EVERY DAY.
(TRY TO COLLECT THIRTY.)

36

THE FIRST THING YOU SEE

START A COLLECTION BASED ON THE FIRST FOUND
OBJECT YOU SEE ON YOUR WALK, WHATEVER
THAT IS. YOU DECIDE WHAT THE CONNECTION
BETWEEN THE OBJECTS IS (CAN BE BASED
ON SHAPE, COLOR, SIZE, ETC.).

↑ THINGS THAT TIE

THE SCULPTOR
HENRY MOORE COLLECTED
BONES, FLINTS, DRIFTWOOD,
SEASHELLS, PEBBLES, WHALE VERTEBRAE,
AND VARIOUS OTHER FOUND OBJECTS;
HE USED ALL OF THESE THINGS AS
SOURCES FOR HIS OWN WORK,
AS WELL AS USING THEM AS
NATURAL SCULPTURES.

IN A 1960S IBM FILM ABOUT THE
COMPUTER THERE IS A GOOD
DESCRIPTION OF THE CREATIVE
PROCESS...
THE NARRATOR STATES THAT THE
ARTIST IS NEVER BORED. SHE LOOKS
AT EVERYTHING AND STORES IT
ALL UP. SHE REJECTS NOTHING;
SHE IS COMPLETELY UNCRITICAL.
WHEN A PROBLEM CONFRONTS HER
SHE GOES THROUGH ALL THE STUFF
SHE HAS COLLECTED, SORTS OUT WHAT
SEEMS TO BE HELPFUL IN THIS
SITUATION, AND RELATES IT IN A
NEW WAY, MAKING A NEW SOLUTION.
SHE PREPARES FOR LEAPS BY
TAKING IN EVERYTHING.

—CORITA KENT

ITEM: CHILDREN'S PLAY STOVE*
MATERIALS: FOUND CARDBOARD, TAPE, PLASTIC
  LIDS, ELECTRICAL TAPE
*ORIGINAL MADE OUT OF WOOD BY GRANDFATHER
                                    CIRCA 1972

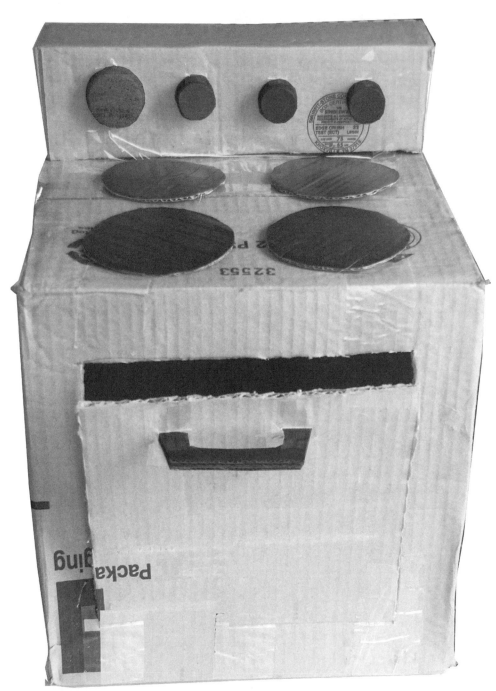

40

ARCHAEOLOGICAL DIG

COLLECT OBJECTS THAT RELATE TO YOUR CHILDHOOD OR INSPIRE MEMORIES. WRITE A BRIEF STORY TO ACCOMPANY EACH OBJECT.

ALTERNATE: RE-CREATE OBJECTS FROM YOUR CHILDHOOD USING FOUND OBJECTS OR READILY AVAILABLE MATERIALS (SUCH AS CARDBOARD, GLUE, STRING, TAPE, LEAVES, WOOD, OR ROCKS). YOU MAY CHOOSE TO RE-CREATE YOUR CHILDHOOD ROOM ON A MINIATURE SCALE USING FOUND MATERIALS.

PLAYING WITH THE SCALE AND MATERIAL OF OBJECTS CAN TRANSFORM THEIR MEANING IN INTERESTING WAYS AND BRING THINGS INTO THE REALM OF IMAGINATION. WHEN WE SEE SOMETHING THAT IS DIFFERENT THAN WE EXPECT WE ARE FORCED TO DEVELOP A NEW RELATIONSHIP WITH IT, ONE THAT ASKS US TO QUESTION "THAT WHICH WE THINK WE KNOW" OR "THAT WHICH WE SEE" WHILE ALSO ADDING A PLAYFUL ELEMENT. TRY PLAYING WITH DIFFERENT MATERIALS TO SEE HOW THE MEANING IS AFFECTED.

1B
blue springs   1592
MY FAVORITE BOWL

1B
ginseng root   386
JEN'S HAIR COLOR

3B
calypso blue   727
THE MAILBOX

1B
sterling   1591
THE HOUSE ON THE CORNER

3B
shaker gray   1594
THE SKY ON 02/02/08

1B
jasper opal   387
MY DESK

3B
olive tree   392
DRIED MOSS IN THE WOODS

1B
spring rain   723
A FOUND TAG

3B △
corn husk   307
DEAD WEEDS

2B
grassy meadows   570
A FOUND TENNIS BALL

2B
heartbeat   1319
BERRIES ON A SHRUB

3B △
florida pink   1320
JUICE LID

1B
you are my sunshine   302
NANA'S HOUSE

1B
yours truly   1317
TREE IN BACKYARD

4B △
ladybug red   1322
MY RED SHOES

3B
four leaf clover   573
MY SCARF

4B △
currant red   1323
WRAPPING PAPER

4B
golden vista   308
SUNSET 01/09/08

42   * PAINT CHIPS COURTESY OF BENJAMIN MOORE

WORLD OF COLOR

COLLECT PAINT CHIPS FROM A PAINT OR HARDWARE STORE. FIND COLORS YOU RESPOND TO IN THE WORLD. ATTEMPT TO MATCH THEM USING THE CHIPS. (YOU CAN ALSO MATCH THE COLORS USING A PORTABLE PAINT SET.) MAKE NOTES OF WHERE YOU SAW THE COLORS.

ALTERNATE: DOCUMENT COLORS FROM YOUR FAVORITE BOOKS, YOUR DREAMS, YOUR MEMORIES.

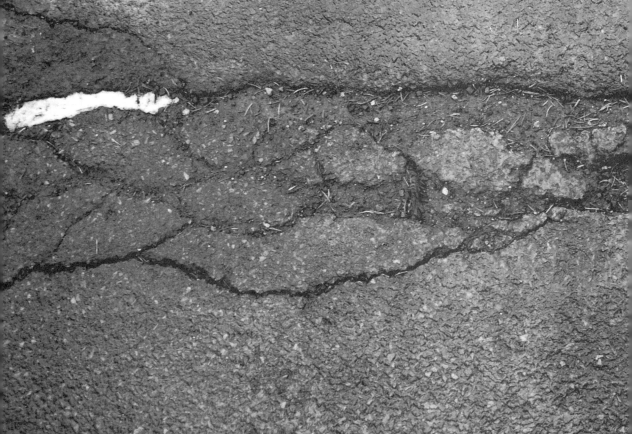

CRACKS

MAP OUT PAVEMENT CRACKS IN YOUR NEIGHBORHOOD.

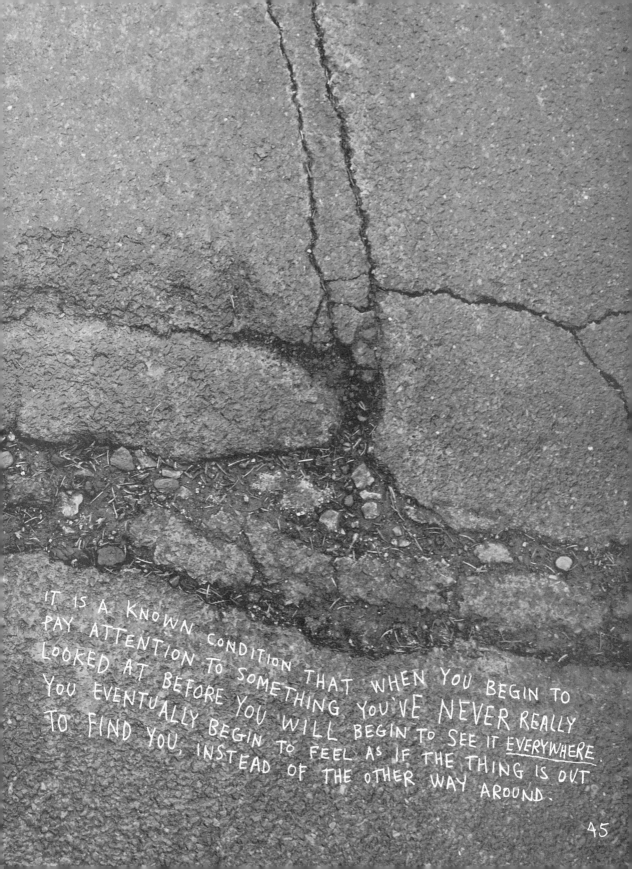

IT IS A KNOWN CONDITION THAT WHEN YOU BEGIN TO
PAY ATTENTION TO SOMETHING YOU'VE NEVER REALLY
LOOKED AT BEFORE YOU WILL BEGIN TO SEE IT EVERYWHERE.
YOU EVENTUALLY BEGIN TO FEEL AS IF THE THING IS OUT
TO FIND YOU, INSTEAD OF THE OTHER WAY AROUND.

45

CASE OF VERY SMALL THINGS

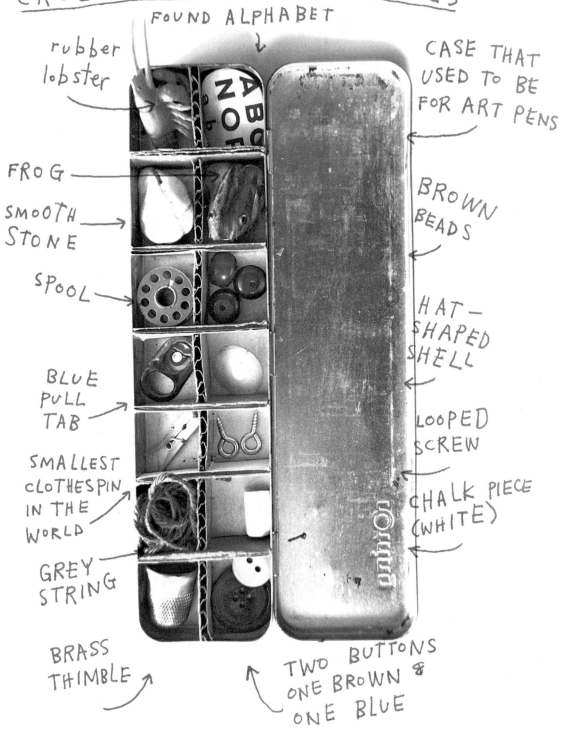

FOUND ALPHABET

rubber lobster

CASE THAT USED TO BE FOR ART PENS

FROG

SMOOTH STONE

BROWN BEADS

SPOOL

HAT-SHAPED SHELL

BLUE PULL TAB

LOOPED SCREW

SMALLEST CLOTHESPIN IN THE WORLD

CHALK PIECE (WHITE)

GREY STRING

BRASS THIMBLE

TWO BUTTONS ONE BROWN & ONE BLUE

CASE OF CURIOSITIES

COLLECT OBJECTS THAT YOU DO NOT UNDERSTAND OR HAVE MEANING FOR.

ALTERNATE: <u>MINIATURE MUSEUM</u>

COLLECT ONLY VERY SMALL THINGS. STORE THEM IN A MINT TIN OR SMALL BOX.

MY DREAM IS TO WALK AROUND THE WORLD. A SMALLISH BACKPACK, ALL ESSENTIALS NEATLY IN PLACE. A CAMERA. A NOTEBOOK. A TRAVELING PAINT SET. A HAT. GOOD SHOES. I DON'T WANT TO TRUDGE UP INSANE MOUNTAINS OR THROUGH WAR-TORN LANDS, JUST A NICE STROLL THROUGH HILL AND DALE. BUT NOW I WALK EVERY WERE IN THE CITY. ANY CITY. YOU SEE EVERYTHING YOU NEED FOR A LIFETIME.
-MAIRA KALMAN

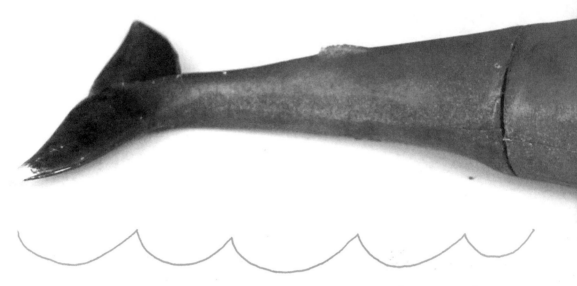

ONE THING

CHOOSE AN EVERYDAY OBJECT. THIS CAN BE SOMETHING YOU FIND ON THE STREET OR SOMETHING YOU HAVE. LOOK AT THE TOP HALF OF THE OBJECT FOR FIFTEEN MINUTES. RECORD EVERYTHING YOU SEE THERE IN DETAIL. THEN DO THE SAME FOR THE BOTTOM HALF. THE LONGER YOU LOOK THE MORE YOU WILL SEE.

* WHALE FOUND ON STREET COVERED IN MUD

IF SOMETHING IS BORING AFTER TWO MINUTES, TRY IT FOR FOUR. IF STILL BORING, THEN EIGHT. THEN SIXTEEN. THEN THIRTY-TWO. EVENTUALLY ONE DISCOVERS THAT IT IS NOT BORING AT ALL. — JOHN CAGE

50

DIFFERENCES

COLLECT MULTIPLES OF ONE THING (SUCH AS LEAVES, STONES, SHELLS, SEEDS, ETC.). LAY THEM OUT IN FRONT OF YOU. OBSERVE THEM IN DETAIL. USING THE "OBJECT LOG," LIST THE DIFFERENCES YOU SEE. TRY TO DOCUMENT AT LEAST TWENTY-FIVE THINGS.

THE IMAGINATION NEEDS MOODLING— LONG, INEFFICIENT HAPPY IDLING, DAWDLING, AND PUTTERING.
— BRENDA UELAND

THE GOGGLES OF ENHANCED PERCEPTION *

* DELUXE MODEL

SHIFTS PERCEPTION OF THE WEARER AND ALLOWS THEM TO SPOT 'NEVER BEFORE SEEN' DETAILS. OF EVERYDAY LIFE.

MATERIALS: CARDBOARD, ELECTRICAL TAPE, METAL WIRE, FOUND PLASTIC TUBE, DUCT TAPE, FOUND ACETATE.

*GOGGLES CAN BE MADE USING ANY VARIETY OF FOUND MATERIALS. NO SPECIAL SKILLS REQUIRED. DESIGN SHOULD BE SUITED TO INDIVIDUAL NEED/TASTE.

FIFTY THINGS

WRITE DOWN (OR DOCUMENT) FIFTY THINGS ABOUT ONE OF THE FOLLOWING: A TRIP TO THE LIBRARY, A TRIP TO THE GROCERY STORE, A WALK IN YOUR NEIGHBORHOOD.

BEFORE FAMILIARITY CAN TURN INTO AWARENESS THE FAMILIAR MUST BE STRIPPED OF ITS INCONSPICUOSNESS; WE MUST GIVE UP ASSUMING THAT THE OBJECT IN QUESTION NEEDS NO EXPLANATION. HOWEVER FREQUENTLY RECURRENT, MODEST, VULGAR IT MAY BE IT WILL NOW BE LABELED AS SOMETHING UNUSUAL.
— BERTOLD BRECHT

·NO· PARKING
FOR 219 RIVER ST. ONLY!
VIOLATORS WILL BE
TOWED AT OWNER'S EXPENSE

REFRESHMENTS

KING
VENETIAN
BLIND
AND
DRAPERY
INC.
MANUFACTURERS

NO
PARKING
LOADING
ZONE

TROY TYPEWRITER & SUP

COLLECTING TYPE

DOCUMENT LETTERING YOU FIND OUT IN THE WORLD. TAKE NOTES ABOUT WHERE AND WHEN YOU FOUND THE SAMPLES.

SOUND MAP

SIT IN A LOCATION FOR ONE HOUR.
DOCUMENT ALL THE SOUNDS YOU CAN
HEAR AND THE TIMES YOU HEARD THEM.
MARK THE APPROXIMATE LOCATION OF THE
SOUNDS IN RELATION TO YOU ON A MAP.

YOU

EXPLORATION # 15

CONSUMER

RECORD EVERYTHING YOU CONSUME <u>OR</u> EVERYTHING YOU PURCHASE IN ONE DAY/ WEEK.

SOURCE: KATE BINGAMAN-BURT

1. IF ON A WINTER'S NIGHT
   A TRAVELER

2. WALT WHITMAN

3. TELEPORTATION

4. SOFT-BOILED EGGS

5. WET EARTH

1. WHAT IS YOUR CURRENT FAVORITE BOOK?   2. WHO WOULD YOU LIKE TO HAVE DINNER WITH?   3. WHAT SUPERHERO POWER WOULD YOU MOST LIKE TO HAVE?   4. WHAT FOOD WOULD YOU EAT EVERYDAY?   5. WHAT IS YOUR FAVORITE SMELL?

SURVEY

CREATE A SIMPLE SURVEY OF
AT LEAST FIVE QUESTIONS.
GIVE IT TO A SAMPLING OF
PEOPLE. DOCUMENT THE
ANSWERS IN A WAY THAT IS
INTERESTING AND READABLE
(FOR INSTANCE, AS A GRAPH,
SPREADSHEET, OR PICTOGRAM).

62

INSTANT SCULPTURE

CONSIDER THAT EVERYTHING AROUND YOU IS A SOURCE FOR SCULPTURE. TRY MAKING QUICK PIECES USING WHATEVER YOU HAVE AROUND YOU IN THE MOMENT.

THAT MOST SORDID OF ALL HAVENS, THE CORNER, DESERVES TO BE EXAMINED. —GASTON BACHELARD

STRUCTURE

DOCUMENT PART OF A BUILDING(S) THAT MOST PEOPLE IGNORE (EXAMPLES INCLUDE THE CEILINGS, BATHROOMS, CORNERS, CLOSETS, AND THE INSIDES OF DRAWERS). PAY ATTENTION TO THE HIDDEN PLACES.

ALTERNATE: DOCUMENT THE CORNERS OF YOUR HOME.

66

FOUND "PAINT"

WHILE ON YOUR TRAVELS, COME UP WITH AS MANY THINGS AS YOU CAN FIND TO USE AS PIGMENT (ADDING WATER IF NECESSARY). SOME EXAMPLES INCLUDE CRUSHED BERRIES, MUD (USING DIFFERENT KINDS OF DIRT), CRUSHED LEAVES, SPICES.

ALTERNATE: DOCUMENT AN EXPERIENCE USING STAINS.

A COLLECTION OF UNCOMMON THINGS

PEA SOUP FOR DINNER

IDEA → FOR A THEME: RANDOM COMBINATION PIECES.

incorporate chance

I'M GETTING HUNGRY. MUST FINISH...

ART MADE BY ACCIDENT

HOW TO CREATE NOTHING?

A BOOK COLLECTION.

BOOKS MADE WITH/FROM FIVE RANDOM ONES WITH

BLUE COVERS. FIND SOMETHING INTERESTING

FROM THE LIBRARY.

THE COLOR GREEN

I AM OBSESSED WITH IT.

if you show people what is in your head they might think you are crazy.

1. CD COVER FOR C.O.

2. WEBSITE FOR W.T.J.

3. NEW SKETCH FOR LITTLE OTSU

4. STUDY.

A SATURATE BRIGHT GREE THE SAME COLOR AS MY PENCIL S

THE LICORICE I BOUGHT

YEARS

NEW

WHO IS T

68

SMALL THOUGHTS

MAKE A LIST OF PLACID SMALL THOUGHTS YOU
HAVE THROUGHOUT THE WEEK (FOR INSTANCE,
WHAT WERE YOU THINKING JUST NOW?).

YOUR FAVORITE STREET

GO TO YOUR FAVORITE STREET. (IF YOU
CAN'T GO THERE PHYSICALLY, THEN
YOU CAN VISIT IT IN YOUR MIND.)
MAP IT OUT ON A PIECE OF PAPER.
THEN DESCRIBE (OR OTHERWISE DOCUMENT)
EVERYTHING IN DETAIL: THE SHOPS, HOUSES,
STREET SIGNS, TREES, ETC.

(BASED ON "THE RUE VILIN" BY GEORGES PEREC)

PEOPLE WATCHING

SIT IN A PUBLIC LOCATION AND DOCUMENT PEOPLE YOU SEE FOR ONE HOUR. TAKE DETAILED NOTES. MAKE SKETCHES OF ONE ITEM THAT STANDS OUT MOST ABOUT EACH PERSON.

ALTERNATE: PEOPLE MAPPING
VISIT A LOCAL PARK OR PUBLIC AREA. CREATE A COLOR-CODED MAP OF THE POSITION OF THE OTHER PEOPLE IN RELATION TO YOU. NOTE WHAT THE PEOPLE LOOKED LIKE (WHAT THEY WERE WEARING).

HOW TO UNCOVER A MYSTERY

1. LET THE MYSTERY FIND YOU—SOMETHING THAT PIQUES YOUR INTEREST AND UNLEASHES YOUR RABID CURIOSITY.

2. RESEARCH. THIS COULD BE CONDUCTED THROUGH A VARIETY OF VENUES (LIBRARY, INTERNET, DICTIONARY, INTERVIEWS, ETC.). DIG UP AS MUCH INFO AS YOU CAN ON THE SUBJECT/EVENT. COLLECT CLUES.

3. FOLLOW ALL "LEADS" (PIECES OF INFO THAT CAUSE YOU TO HEAD IN NEW DIRECTIONS). CONTACT PEOPLE INVOLVED.

4. GET INVOLVED DIRECTLY WITH THE THING YOU ARE RESEARCHING (FOR EXAMPLE, TAKE A CLASS, WRITE EXPERTS, ETC.).

5. CONDUCT A RE-CREATION (OF AN OBJECT OR EVENT). USE MAPS, DIORAMAS, PHOTOS, DIAGRAMS, ETC. LOOK AT THE SITUATION FROM DIFFERENT ANGLES.

COMBINATIONS

COMBINE GROUPS OF OBJECTS FOR VISUAL OR EMOTIONAL CONTRAST. YOU MIGHT TRY NATURAL VS. HUMAN-MADE, CONTRASTING COLORS, ALIVE VS. DECAYING, LIGHT VS. DARK.

ALTERNATE #1: TAKE TWO DIFFERENT OBJECTS AND TRY TO CREATE AS MANY CONNECTIONS BETWEEN THEM AS YOU CAN. YOU MAY NEED TO RESEARCH THEM TO COME UP WITH MORE IDEAS.

ALTERNATE #2: WRITE ABOUT WHAT IT IS LIKE TO COMBINE TWO DIFFERENT ACTIVITIES, SUCH AS EATING AND READING, OR WALKING AND DRAWING. HOW DOES ONE ACTIVITY AFFECT THE OTHER?

WATER

STUDY AND DOCUMENT SHAPES MADE BY WATER. FIND AS MANY AS YOU CAN. RESEARCH SHAPES MADE BY WATER. COME UP WITH NEW ONES.

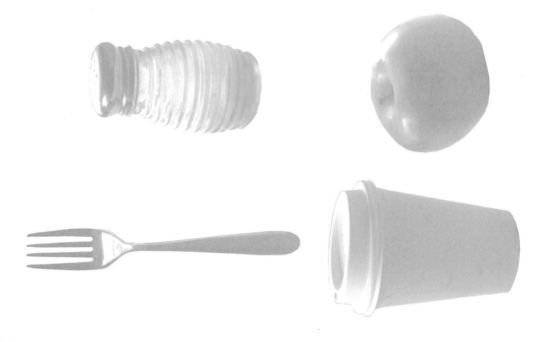

BECOMING LEONARD COHEN*

SKETCH OR DOCUMENT THINGS THAT YOU USE IN YOUR DAILY ROUTINE.

* MUSICIAN LEONARD COHEN DOES THIS REGULARLY AS A FORM OF MEDITATIVE PRACTICE.

I HAVE ALWAYS LOVED THINGS,
JUST THINGS IN THE WORLD.
I LOVE TRYING TO FIND THE
SHAPE OF THINGS.
— LEONARD COHEN

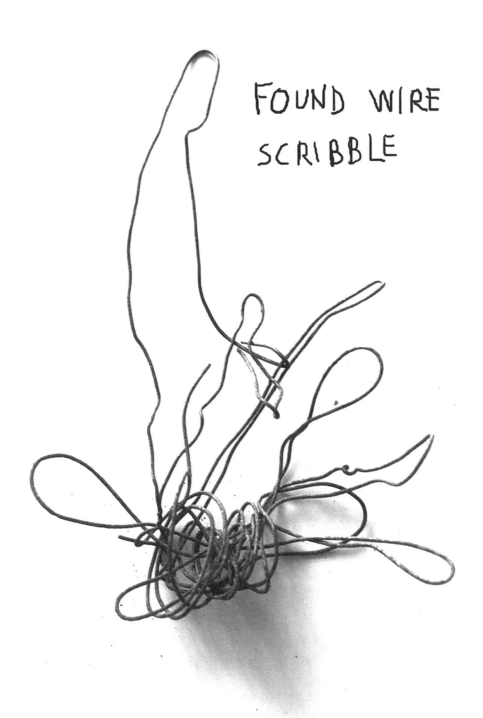

FOUND WIRE
SCRIBBLE

82

ACCIDENTAL ART

GO FOR A WALK. IDENTIFY AND DOCUMENT EXISTING "ART" THAT YOU FIND, SUCH AS THINGS THAT ARE NOT CREATED ON PURPOSE. SOME EXAMPLES INCLUDE STAINS ON THE SIDEWALK, SPILLED PAINT, BIRD POO, RESIDUE, CORROSION, RUST, THINGS THAT ARE DAMAGED, RANDOM ARRANGEMENTS OF OBJECTS THAT YOU FIND INTERESTING, A BAG CAUGHT IN A TREE.

LOOK WITH ALL YOUR EYES. LOOK.
— JULES VERNE

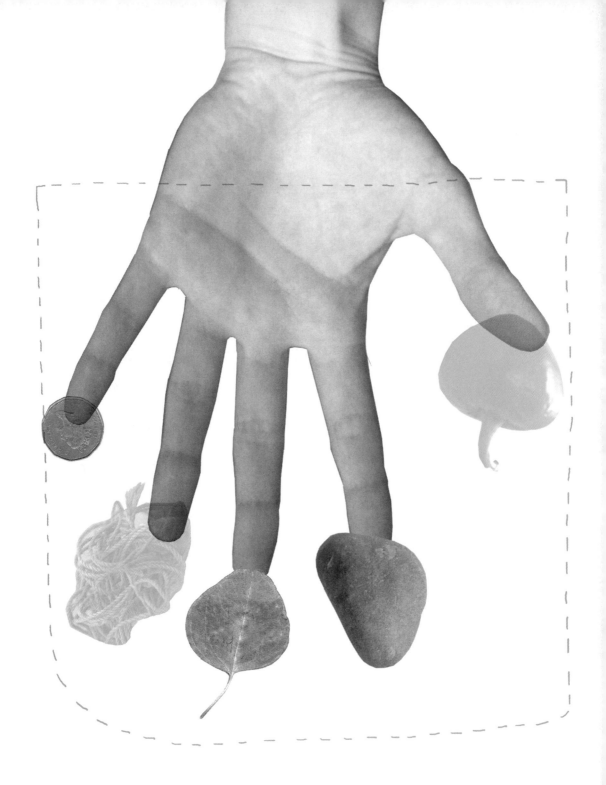

84

BLIND OBSERVATION

PLACE AN OBJECT OR A SERIES OF OBJECTS IN YOUR POCKET. DESCRIBE THEM USING ONLY TOUCH. ALTERNATE: GO AROUND YOUR ROOM IN THE DARK AND IDENTIFY ALL THE OBJECTS IN IT BY TOUCH. DESCRIBE THEM.

TACTILE BOARDS

COLLECT MATERIALS BASED ON TEXTURE.
GLUE THE TEXTURES TO A SHEET OF PAPER
OR CARDBOARD (SEE DIAGRAM BELOW). INVITE
PEOPLE TO CLOSE THEIR EYES AND GUESS
WHAT THE DIFFERENT MATERIALS ARE.
EXPERIMENT WITH TOUCHING THE BOARDS
USING DIFFERENT PARTS OF YOUR BODY (SUCH
AS YOUR CHEEK OR ELBOW). ALTERNATE #1:
CREATE A TACTILE "MAP" OF A PLACE
USING TEXTURES TO REPRESENT THE
DIFFERENT AREAS OR QUALITIES.

ALTERNATE #2: USING A NON-
DRYING CLAY (PLASTICINE), CREATE
RELIEFS BY PRESSING THE CLAY
INTO DIFFERENT TEXTURES YOU
FIND.

SOURCE: BRUNO MUNARI

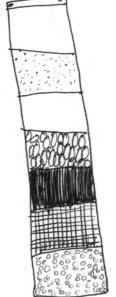

TRAVEL HISTORY

COLLECT OBJECTS THAT TELL A
STORY OF YOUR TRAVELS. DOCUMENT
WHERE YOU FOUND EACH OBJECT.

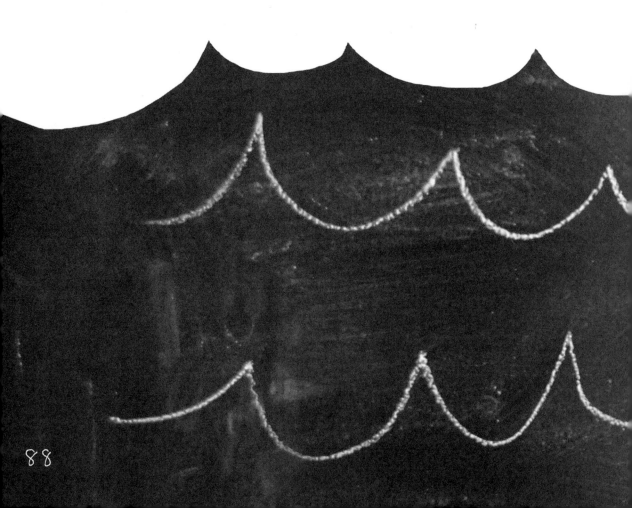

ALTERNATE #2: WHAT ABOUT CREATING SOUNDS WITH OTHER ITEMS SUCH AS FOOD? WHAT SOUNDS CAN YOU MAKE USING FRUIT AND VEGETABLES?
RESEARCH: THE VEGETABLE ORCHESTRA

90

FOUND SOUNDS

COLLECT OBJECTS BASED ON THE SOUNDS YOU
CAN MAKE WITH THEM (FOR EXAMPLE, TUBES, METAL,
PLASTIC). YOU MAY WANT TO EXPERIMENT WITH
ADDING OR COMBINING OBJECTS TO MAKE
NEW SOUNDS, OR ADDING OTHER ELEMENTS
(LIKE WATER). CONSIDER THAT WE
EXPERIENCE SOUND IN ALL
PARTS OF OUR BODY, NOT
JUST OUR EARS. (WE CAN
FEEL VIBRATIONS.)

SOURCE: EVELYN GLENNIE

ALTERNATE #1:
TAKE A FIELD TRIP
SPECIFICALLY TO
LISTEN TO AND
DOCUMENT SOUNDS.
SOURCE: MAX NEUHAUS

NOW I WILL DO NOTHING
BUT **LISTEN**.

I HEAR ALL SOUNDS RUNNING
TOGETHER, COMBINED, FUSED, OR FOLLOWING,
SOUNDS OF THE CITY, AND SOUNDS OUT OF
THE CITY — SOUNDS OF THE DAY AND NIGHT...
— WALT WHITMAN

OFFICIAL LICENSE TO

CREATE YOUR OWN REALITY.

NAME: _ _ _ _ _ _ _ _ _ _ _ _ _ _

ADDRESS: _ _ _ _ _ _ _ _ _ _ _ _ _

EXPERIMENTING SINCE:

AFFIX
PHOTO
HERE

_ _ _ _ _ _ _ _ _ _ _

OFFICIAL
STAMP

* CUT OUT AND CARRY WITH YOU.

WORLD OF MAGIC

COLLECT OBJECTS FOR THEIR POTENTIAL
MAGIC QUALITY. ATTACH A STORY
TO THEM. OR CREATE A FICTITIOUS
HISTORY ABOUT THE OBJECT.

MAGIC PINECONE
WHEN PLANTED
GROWS A TREE
THAT CAUSES ALL
WHO SIT UNDER
IT TO FALL
ASLEEP AND HAVE
VIVID DREAMS.

93

WHEN I'M WORKING WITH A MATERIAL, IT'S NOT JUST THE STONE [THAT] I'M TRYING TO UNDERSTAND, NOT A SINGLE ISOLATED OBJECT BUT NATURE AS A WHOLE— HOW THE LEAF HAS GROWN, HOW IT HAS CHANGED, HOW IT HAS DECAYED, HOW THE WEATHER IS AFFECTED BY IT. BY WORKING WITH A LEAF IN IT'S PLACE I BEGIN TO UNDERSTAND THESE PROCESSES.

— ANDY GOLDSWORTHY

94

ARRANGEMENTS

GO OUT AND COLLECT ANY ITEM YOU CAN FIND IN ABUNDANCE (LEAVES WORK WELL FOR THIS IN THE FALL). BRING THEM HOME AND COME UP WITH AS MANY DIFFERENT WAYS OF DISPLAYING AND ARRANGING THEM AS POSSIBLE. TRY TO THINK OF THINGS YOU'VE NEVER CONSIDERED BEFORE (SUCH AS SEALING THEM IN ICE, COVERING BOOK COVERS WITH THEM, MAKING A LONG CHAIN THAT REACHES THE LENGTH OF YOUR HOUSE, ETC.). REALLY EXPLORE THE MATERIAL AND TRY TO UNDERSTAND IT, HOW IT WORKS, HOW IT IS AFFECTED BY DIFFERENT FACTORS (MOVEMENT, HUMIDITY, WEIGHT). EXPERIMENT WITH ARRANGEMENTS THAT THE VIEWER CAN PHYSICALLY INTERACT WITH (MAKE A TUNNEL, A WEB, A HOUSE). TRY ADDING OTHER MATERIALS (WATER, DIRT, OR PAINT).

envel

51

World Premiere at the Palm Springs
International Festival of Short Films,
Wednesday, ~~~~~ at 5pm.

96

INTERESTING GARBAGE

COLLECT PIECES OF DETRITUS YOU
FIND INTERESTING OR INTRIGUING.
DOCUMENT THEM IN SOME WAY,
WITH SKETCHES, PHOTOGRAPHS, OR
WRITINGS. TAKE NOTE OF WHERE
AND WHEN THE ITEMS WERE FOUND.
SOME THINGS TO PONDER: WHAT IS
THE DIFFERENCE BETWEEN WHAT
WE CHOOSE TO KEEP AND WHAT
WE THROW AWAY? IS WHAT WE
CONSIDER 'WITHOUT USE' MEANINGLESS?
HOW CAN WE FIND NEW PRESENTATIONS
FOR THESE THINGS?
SOURCE: CANDY JERNIGAN

STORIES ABOUT PLACE ARE MAKESHIFT
THINGS. THEY ARE COMPOSED WITH THE
WORLD'S DEBRIS.   — MICHEL DE CERTEAU

SECRET PORTAL

INVISIBLE CITY

USING YOUR IMAGINATION,
CREATE A PORTRAIT OF YOUR
CITY OR TOWN IN WHICH EVERYTHING
THAT YOU ENCOUNTER IS MAGICAL,
EXAGGERATED, OR SLIGHTLY ALTERED
FROM REALITY. USE WHATEVER DOCUMENTATION
METHOD YOU PREFER.

SOURCE: INVISIBLE
CITIES, BY ITALO
CALVINO

THE WORLD IS AN ASTONISHING PLACE.
- MILTON GLASER

EXPLORATION #36

THE TRUTH ABOUT INANIMATE OBJECTS

CAPTURE THE HIDDEN LIFE OF INANIMATE OBJECTS YOU FIND OUT IN THE WORLD. WHAT DO THEY DO WHEN THERE ARE NO PEOPLE AROUND? TRACK THEIR ACTIVITIES AND SOCIAL INTERACTIONS. YOU MAY HAVE TO GO UNDERCOVER FOR THIS OPERATION.

SOURCE: SKINNY LEGS AND ALL, BY TOM ROBBINS

THE UNIVERSE IS THE MIRROR IN WHICH WE
CAN CONTEMPLATE ONLY WHAT WE HAVE
LEARNED TO KNOW IN OURSELVES.
— M.R. PALOMAR,
BY ITALO CALVINO

TIME OBSERVATION

COME UP WITH SEVERAL WAYS OF DOCUMENTING THE PASSAGE OF TIME, BASED ON WHERE YOU ARE SITTING.

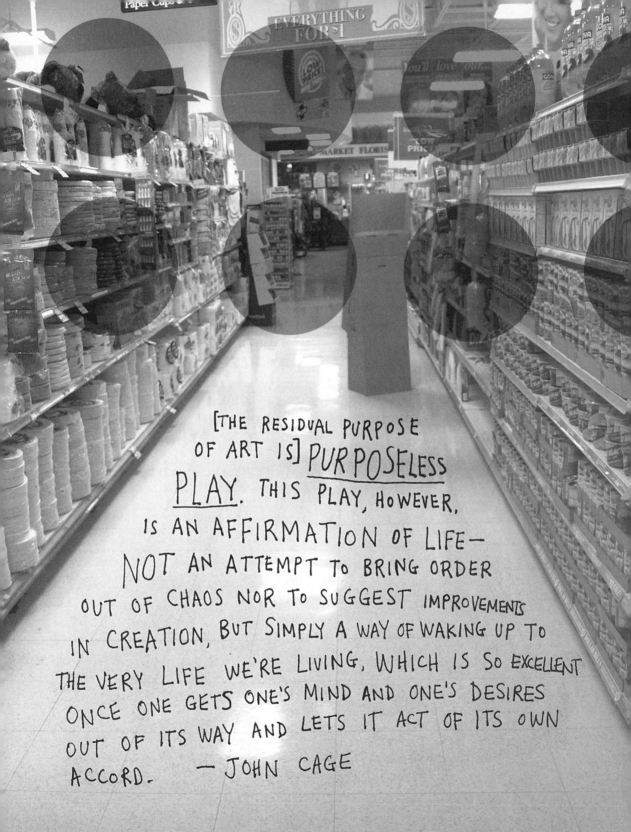

[THE RESIDUAL PURPOSE
OF ART IS] PURPOSELESS
PLAY. THIS PLAY, HOWEVER,
IS AN AFFIRMATION OF LIFE—
NOT AN ATTEMPT TO BRING ORDER
OUT OF CHAOS NOR TO SUGGEST IMPROVEMENTS
IN CREATION, BUT SIMPLY A WAY OF WAKING UP TO
THE VERY LIFE WE'RE LIVING, WHICH IS SO EXCELLENT
ONCE ONE GETS ONE'S MIND AND ONE'S DESIRES
OUT OF ITS WAY AND LETS IT ACT OF ITS OWN
ACCORD. — JOHN CAGE

GROCERY SHOPPING WITH JOHN CAGE

COLLECT THINGS IN YOUR BASKET BASED ON ONE VARIABLE OF YOUR CHOOSING (SUCH AS COLOR, SHAPE, SIZE, PACKAGING, FOODS YOU'VE NEVER EATEN, THINGS YOU DON'T UNDERSTAND, FOODS THAT ARE FLAT, ETC.). YOU DO NOT HAVE TO PURCHASE THEM UNLESS YOU WANT TO. DOCUMENT THEM SOMEHOW.

ALTERNATE: MAKE A LIST OF VARIOUS ITEMS (SUCH AS EVERY KIND OF CHEESE THE STORE SELLS). CHECK OFF THE ONES YOU'VE TRIED. DO A QUICK SKETCH OF THE SHAPES THEY COME IN.

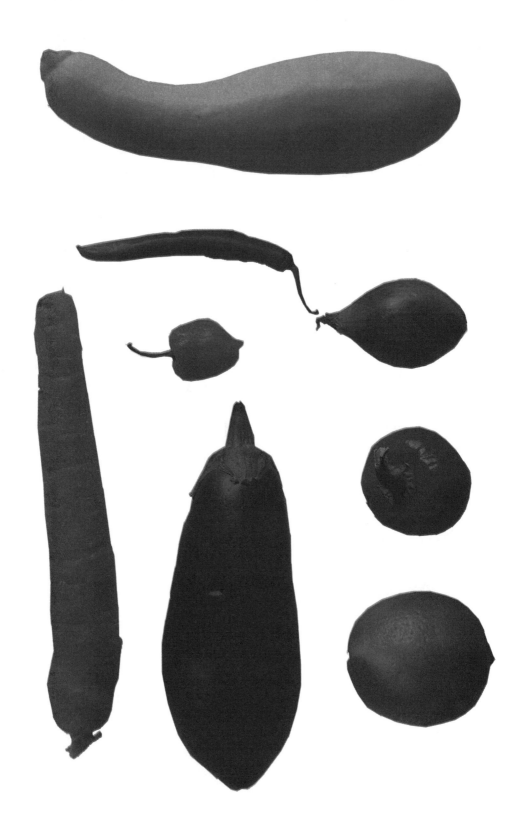

106

FOOD AS ART

PREPARE A MEAL PAYING CLOSE ATTENTION TO ALL THE DETAILS. DOCUMENT THE PROCESS IN SOME FORM. INCORPORATE ALL THE SENSES IN YOUR PROCESS. SHARE THE MEAL WITH SOMEONE. SUGGESTION: USING THE EXPERIENCE LOG, TAKE AN ETHNOGRAPHIC APPROACH (PRETEND IT'S THE FIRST TIME YOU'VE DONE IT).

SOURCE: RIRKRIT TIRAVANIJA

ALTERED

FIND A WAY TO ALTER YOUR PHYSICAL EXPERIENCE OF THE WORLD (YOUR SENSES) WHILE ON YOUR TRAVELS. EXAMPLES ARE SQUINTING YOUR EYES TO BLUR YOUR VISION, WEARING COLOR-TINTED GLASSES, CLOSING ONE EYE, WEARING EARPLUGS, HANGING UPSIDE DOWN FOR A TIME, WALKING AS SLOWLY AS POSSIBLE, AND PLUGGING YOUR NOSE WHILE EATING.

DOCUMENT THE EXPERIENCE.

STATES

ANECDOTE: I HAD A TEACHER IN ART SCHOOL WHO TURNED EVERYTHING HE LOOKED AT UPSIDE DOWN. EVERYTHING. IT WAS AS IF HE COULD SEE IT BETTER THAT WAY. IF HE COULDN'T MOVE IT, HE WOULD GET ON HIS HANDS AND KNEES AND TURN HIMSELF UPSIDE DOWN. OFTEN WE FORGET ABOUT THE PHYSICALITY OF OBSERVING, LITERALLY CHANGING OUR VIEWPOINT OR PERSPECTIVE.

EXPLORATION #41

FOUND FACES

DOCUMENT ANY NATURALLY OCCURRING
FACES YOU FIND ON YOUR TRAVELS.
LOOK FOR THEM IN PLUMBING PARTS,
FIXTURES (DOOR HOOKS), IN NATURE (TREES),
IN HUMAN-MADE OBJECTS, IN THE
CLOUDS, ETC.

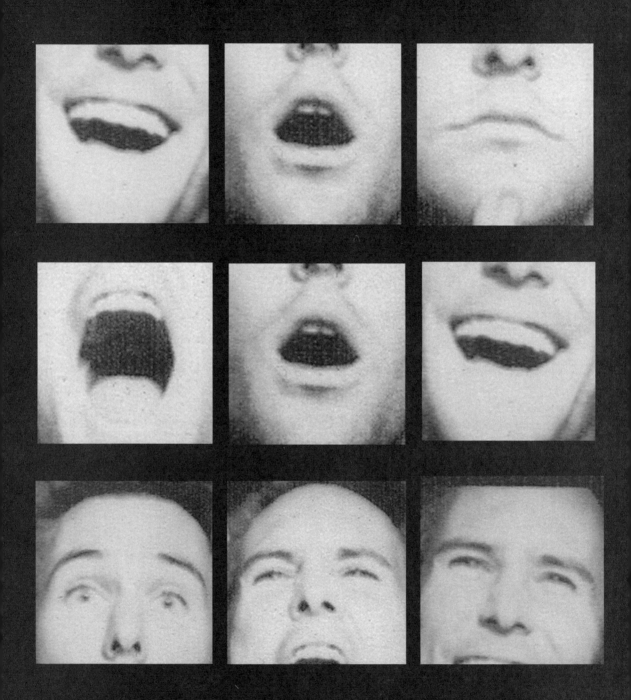

LOCAL LORE

Document a place by interviewing people about it. You can transcribe by using some kind of recording equipment or by filling out an experience documentation log.

Source: Harrell Fletcher

12" BASK... weern

Hick...

20
ist überall der klei-
ne Kavalier der
Französin Yvonne.

114

FOUND PAPER*

ONE OF THE EASIEST THINGS TO FIND IN THE WORLD IS DISCARDED PAPER. WHILE ONE LONE ITEM MAY NOT SEEM TERRIBLY INTERESTING, WHEN YOU START TO ASSEMBLE A COLLECTION, IT CAN BE INTENSELY SATISFYING TO LOOK AT AND ARRANGE INTO DIFFERENT CONFIGURATIONS.

* NOTE: FOUND CARDBOARD PROVIDES ENDLESS POSSIBILITIES FOR CREATIVE PRODUCTION. ALWAYS HAVE SOME ON HAND FOR SPONTANEOUS PROJECTS.

* GLUE ENVELOPE HERE FOR COLLECTION PURPOSES.

DA COSA NASCE COSA.
(ONE THING LEADS TO ANOTHER.)
— BRUNO MUNARI

DATE DUE

LIBRARY EXPLORATION

CHOOSE ONE ITEM OR THEME.
YOU MAY USE PAGE 23 FOR IDEAS
(THINGS TO DOCUMENT OR COLLECT).
GO TO A LIBRARY. CONDUCT
RESEARCH ON YOUR CHOSEN
ITEM USING THE OBJECT LOG.

COLLECT AS MANY DIFFERENT
MATERIALS AS YOU CAN TO DISPLAY
LATER, SUCH AS SKETCHES,
HISTORY, NOTES, DRAWINGS, AND
PHOTOS. PRESENT YOUR FINDINGS
AS AN INSTALLATION.

ALTERNATE: CREATE POEMS
BASED ON THE TITLES OF BOOKS.
(BASED ON THE WORK OF NINA
KATCHADOURIAN)

WHAT WE NEED TO QUESTION IS BRICKS, CONCRETE, GLASS, OUR TABLE MANNERS, OUR UTENSILS, OUR TOOLS, THE WAY WE SPEND OUR TIME, OUR RHYTHMS. TO QUESTION THAT WHICH SEEMS TO HAVE CEASED FOREVER TO ASTONISH US. WE LIVE, TRUE, WE BREATHE, TRUE; WE WALK, WE OPEN DOORS, WE GO DOWN STAIRCASES, WE SIT AT A TABLE IN ORDER TO EAT, WE LIE DOWN ON A BED IN ORDER TO SLEEP. HOW? WHY? WHERE? WHEN? WHY? — GEORGES PEREC

SELF-ETHNO

USE YOURSELF AS YOUR SUBJECT FOR DOCUMENTATION. DOCUMENT IN DETAIL ALL OF YOUR MOVEMENTS, ACTIVITIES, BEHAVIORS, AND CONVERSATIONS THROUGHOUT THE COURSE OF A WEEK. INCLUDE DATE, TIME, & PLACE.

ETHNOGRAPHY. N. THE DOCUMENTATION AND ANALYSIS OF A PARTICULAR CULTURE THROUGH FIELD RESEARCH.

SELF-ETHNOGRAPHY. N. THE DOCUMENTATION AND ANALYSIS OF THE SELF AS A FOREIGN CULTURE THROUGH FIELD RESEARCH.

GRAPHY

ALTERNATE: CHOOSE ONE SPECIFIC ASPECT OF YOUR EXISTENCE TO DOCUMENT (E.G., DETERMINE HOW MANY STEPS YOU TAKE ON A DAILY BASIS).

FOUND PATTERNS

COLLECT OR DOCUMENT AS MANY PATTERNS AS YOU CAN FIND WHILE ON YOUR TRAVELS. YOU MAY DECIDE TO USE ONLY PATTERNS IN NATURE, OR HUMAN-MADE, OR BOTH. PENCIL RUBBINGS WORK WELL FOR THIS.

NO MAN WHO EVER LIVED LIKED SO MANY THINGS AND DISLIKED SO FEW AS WALT WHITMAN. ALL NATURAL OBJECTS SEEMED TO HAVE A CHARM FOR HIM. ALL SIGHTS AND SOUNDS SEEMED TO PLEASE HIM.

-DR. WILLIAM JAMES, THE VARIETIES OF RELIGIOUS EXPERIENCE

THE SHAPES OF STAINS AND SPLOTCHES

MAKE TRACINGS OF STAINS OR SPLOTCHES YOU FIND. MAKE NOTES ABOUT WHERE YOU FOUND THEM. WORK IN DIFFERENT COLORS. TRY CUTTING THE SHAPES OUT OF PAPER AND LAYERING THEM TO MAKE A COLLAGE.

SOURCE: INGRID CALAME

WHO IS TO SAY THAT PLEASURE IS USELESS?
- CHARLES EAMES

FINDER EXPLORATION

USING THE FINDER BELOW, GO OUT INTO THE WORLD AND CREATE A PAGE OF QUICK SKETCHES DOCUMENTING DIFFERENT COMPOSITIONS. CHOOSE COMPOSITIONS WHERE YOU CANNOT TELL WHAT THE SUBJECT MATTER IS. ALTERNATE: DO THIS EXERCISE USING A CAMERA.

CUT OUT.

DIRECTIONS

1. TRACE FINDER ONTO CARDSTOCK.
2. CUT OUT.

ALTERNATE:

1. JUST CUT OUT MIDDLE HOLE.
2. CARRY THE BOOK WITH YOU ON YOUR EXCURSIONS.

125

I READ IN THE PAPER THE OTHER DAY THAT SCIENTISTS HAVE DISCOVERED THE MEANING OF LIFE.*

WHAT WAS IT?

I FORGET.

* CONVERSATION BORROWED FROM KURT VONNEGUT'S CAT'S CRADLE

126

EXPLORATION #49

FOUND WORDS

USING THE EXPERIENCE LOG, DOCUMENT AN OVERHEARD CONVERSATION. ALTERNATE: COLLECT WORDS YOU FIND INTERESTING.

DURING HIS STAY IN LONDON IN 1874, THE FRENCH POET RIMBAUD COLLECTED ENGLISH WORD-LISTS. STRINGS OF ENGLISH WORDS, SOMETIMES HYPHENATED, WERE COLLECTED IN HIS PAPERS. ON "PIGEONS" FOR EXAMPLE, HE LISTS "HOMING-WORKING-FANTAILS-PEARL-EYED TUMBLER..." THE LIST OF WORDS GOES ON AND TUMBLES IN A VERTIGINOUS SPIRAL OF SOUNDS. —BRIONY FER

127

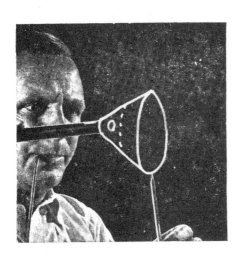

SUBJECT IS WEARING
A "SMELL LOCATOR" DEVICE.

ONCE A SMELL IS LOCATED
A HONING BEACON IS
ACTIVATED ALLOWING
SUBJECT TO LOCATE THE
SOURCE.

FOUND SMELLS

GO FOR A WALK. MAKE A LIST
OF ALL THE SMELLS IN YOUR
NEIGHBORHOOD. BE AS DETAILED
AS POSSIBLE. ATTEMPT TO
IDENTIFY SOURCES.

PET PEEVES
PREFERENCES
QUESTIONS
QUOTIDIAN (EVERYDAY)
RANDOM THOUGHTS
REGRETS
RELATIONSHIPS
SCHOOL
SOCIAL LIFE
SPIRITUALITY
SUCCESSES
SYNCHRONICITY
TOYS
VACATIONS
WALKS
WORK

DYSFUNCTION
ECCENTRICITIES
HUMOR
IDIOSYNCRASIES
ILLNESS
INSECURITIES
LESSONS
LOVES
LUNCH
MEMORIES
MISTAKES
MISUNDERSTANDING
MOODS
NATURE
NEUROSIS
NEIGHBORHOOD
OBSERVATIONS
PASSIONS

EXERCISE
FACE
FALL
FAMILY
FAVORITES
FEARS
FOOD
FRIENDS
FRUSTRATIONS
FURNITURE
GIFTS
GRATITUDE
HOBBIES
HOUSE

ADDICTIONS
ADVENTURES
AVERSIONS
ANIMALS
BOOKS
BODY
BLUNDERS
BREAKFAST
CHILDHOOD
CLOTHING
CLIMATE
COINCIDENCES
DECISIONS
DISLIKES
DISASTERS
DREAMS

130

NON-LINEAR LIFE

DOCUMENT YOUR ACTIVITIES FROM ONE DAY/WEEK/MONTH/YEAR IN AN ENCYCLOPEDIC FASHION.
ALTERNATE: CREATE ICONS FOR YOUR LIFE ACTIVITIES. DOCUMENT THEM ON A CHART. TRY CHANGING THE ORDER OF THINGS.

CLOSE OBSERVATION OF A
SINGLE SUBJECT, WHETHER
IT IS AS TINY AS PASTEUR'S
MICROBES OR AS GREAT AS
EINSTEIN'S UNIVERSE, IS THE
KIND OF WORK THAT HAPPENS
LESS AND LESS THESE DAYS.
GLUED TO COMPUTER AND TV
SCREENS, WE HAVE FORGOTTEN
HOW TO LOOK AT THE NATURAL
WORLD. THE ORIGINAL INSTRUCTOR
ON HOW TO BE CURIOUS ABOUT DETAIL.
— JENNIFER NEW

138

MINIATURE ECOSYSTEM

COLLECT WATER FROM THREE DIFFERENT SITES. THESE CAN INCLUDE A LAKE, POND, STREAM, PUDDLE, OR SIMILAR. COMBINE THE SAMPLES IN A JAR WITH A TIGHT FITTING LID. PLACE THE JAR IN A SUNNY LOCATION AND WATCH TO SEE THE ECOSYSTEM UNFOLD. SOON THIS MINIATURE WORLD WILL START TO ORGANIZE ITSELF AND CREATE SOME INTERESTING RESULTS. MAKE NOTES ABOUT THE DAILY CHANGES. EXPERIMENT WITH DIFFERENT WATER SOURCES TO SEE HOW THE RESULTS VARY. EACH ECOSYSTEM IS UNIQUE.

SOURCE: <u>GAIA'S GARDEN</u>, BY TOBY HEMENWAY

135

CHOPSTICK ↘

STICK ↗

TWINE ↘

RUSTY NAIL ↗

PINE BOUGH ↘

136

FOUND WRITING UTENSILS

EXPERIMENT WITH AS MANY DIFFERENT KINDS OF WRITING UTENSILS AS YOU CAN. YOU MAY USE FOUND PAINT, INK, OR REGULAR PAINT.

SOMETIMES A TREE CAN TELL YOU MORE THAN CAN BE READ IN A BOOK.

—CARL JUNG

THE LANGUAGE OF TREES

COLLECT AS MANY PARTS OF TREES AS YOU CAN. (USE THINGS THAT HAVE FALLEN NATURALLY, YOU DON'T WANT TO HARM THE TREES.) ARRANGE YOUR COLLECTION. PLAY WITH IT. HANG IT. STUDY THE SHAPES. DO DRAWINGS. HANG THINGS FROM BRANCHES. CELEBRATE TREES!

LIFE IS A DICTIONARY. — RALPH WALDO EMERSON

WAYS TO TRANSFORM AN EVERYDAY EXPERIENCE

LOOK AT THE WORLD AS A PUZZLE THAT YOU DETERMINE THE MEANING OF.

ADD MUSIC
(WITH HEADPHONES). SET A TONE DETERMINED BY YOU.

SEE EVERYTHING AS A FILM. YOU ARE THE FILMMAKER. EVERYTHING IS A SOURCE.

MAKE A MOVIE WITH YOUR EYES.

INVOKE THE IMAGINATION (PRETEND YOU ARE ON A SECRET MISSION, GO INTO CHARACTER, PERCEIVE INANIMATE OBJECTS AS REAL).

PRETEND YOU ARE SOMEONE ELSE. "WHAT WOULD ——— DO?"

ATTEMPT TO SEE THINGS FROM AS MANY ANGLES AS POSSIBLE.

ALTER YOUR HABITUAL ROUTINE. TAKE A DIFFERENT ROUTE THAN YOU NORMALLY WOULD.

WEAR A COSTUME OR DISGUISE.

141

WHAT TO COLLECT	WHERE TO EXPLORE	METHOD OF INVESTIGATION	DOCUMENTING METHOD

HOW TO INCORPORATE INDETERMINACY

ALLOW SOMETHING (OR SOMEONE) ELSE TO CHOOSE WHAT DIRECTION YOU HEAD IN, OR WHAT OR HOW YOU EXPLORE.

THE EXPLORER GAME

WHAT YOU WILL NEED: SCISSORS, A VESSEL OF SOME KIND (BOWL OR POCKET)

DIRECTIONS

1. USING THE GRID PROVIDED FILL IN AS MANY VARIABLES AS YOU WISH IN EACH CATEGORY.

2. CUT OUT THE SQUARES. KEEP THE CATEGORIES SEPARATE.

3. PLACE THEM IN SOME KIND OF VESSEL.

4. WITHOUT LOOKING, MIX THEM UP AND PICK ONE FROM EACH CATEGORY.

5. EXPLORE USING THESE VARIABLES.

WHAT IF MY HOUSE WERE A PLAYGROUND? A BLANK CANVAS? HAD SECRET POWERS?

WHAT IF ALL MY NEIGHBORS HAD SECRET LIVES?

THOUGHT EXPERIMENTS

EINSTEIN USED "THOUGHT EXPERIMENTS" (QUESTIONS THAT CAN ONLY BE SOLVED USING THE IMAGINATION), ON A REGULAR BASIS. HE ACTUALLY FORMULATED THE SPECIAL THEORY OF RELATIVITY BY ASKING THE QUESTION, "WHAT WOULD IT BE LIKE TO TRAVEL ON A BEAM OF LIGHT?" IT IS INTERESTING TO CONDUCT THESE THOUGHT EXPERIMENTS IN THE MIDST OF EVERYDAY LIFE.

144

145

SECRET EXPLORER UNIFORM *

* COMPLETE WITH HIDDEN INTERIOR POCKETS FOR CARRYING FINDS

PENS

TOP SECRET

MAGNIFYING GLASS

NOTEBOOK

VARIOUS COLLECTED ITEMS

I AM WHAT IS AROUND ME. — WALLACE STEVENS

SCAVENGER HUNT COLLECTION

MAKE A LIST OF THINGS TO FIND IN ONE DAY. THIS IS FUN TO DO WITH A FRIEND OR IN A GROUP, AND THEN COMPARE YOUR FINDINGS.

SOME IDEAS:

o AN ENVELOPE THAT HAS BEEN PREVIOUSLY MAILED

o A PIECE OF A PUZZLE

o SOMETHING THAT WAS GROWING

o AN OVERHEARD STORY

o A FOOTPRINT

o A MATCH BOOK

o SOMETHING THAT IS OR WAS MEANINGFUL TO SOMEONE ELSE

o A SMELL

o SOMETHING THAT IS BLUE

THE IMPORTANCE OF GETTING LOST

THE CLOSER MAN GETS TO THE UNKNOWN, THE
MORE INVENTIVE HE BECOMES — THE QUICKER
HE ADOPTS NEW WAYS.   —BUCKMINSTER FULLER

TO ENTER INTO THE UNKNOWN (TO PARTAKE
IN AN EXPERIMENT) INVOLVES A WILLINGNESS
TO FULLY EXPERIENCE AND STUDY THINGS WE
DON'T UNDERSTAND, AND TO EMBRACE THAT
LACK OF UNDERSTANDING.

THERE ARE DIFFERENT WAYS OF "GETTING
LOST." THERE IS THE LITERAL LOST, AS IN
BEING LOST IN THE WOODS UNABLE TO FIND YOUR
WAY BACK TO THE STARTING POINT. OR THERE
ARE METAPHORICAL EXAMPLES OF BEING LOST:
LOST IN ONE'S HEAD, A LOST SOUL, LOST IN
TIME. IN THE CONTEXT OF EXPLORING WE
CAN THINK OF IT IN TERMS OF "EXISTING
IN A STATE WHERE YOU DO NOT KNOW EXACTLY
WHERE YOU ARE HEADED." IN THIS SENSE WE
MAY CHOOSE TO BECOME EITHER LITERALLY LOST,
EXPLORING A PLACE WE'VE NEVER BEEN BEFORE,
OR LOST IN THE SENSE THAT WE ENTER INTO A
RELATIONSHIP WITH OBJECTS AND IDEAS WITHOUT
KNOWING WHAT THE OUTCOME WILL BE.

HOW TO WANDER AIMLESSLY

1. PICK A DAY AND TIME.

2. PACK A BAG. ⟶

3. START HEADING IN ANY DIRECTION. ACT ONLY ON INSTINCT.

4. DO THE OPPOSITE OF WHAT YOU THINK YOU SHOULD.

5. IF YOU START TO THINK YOU ARE WASTING YOUR TIME THEN YOU ARE DOING IT CORRECTLY.

6. KEEP GOING. PAY ATTENTION TO THE DETAILS. LOSE ALL SENSE OF TIME AND PLACE.

150

FIELD WORK

SPACE IN WHICH TO CONDUCT YOUR OBSERVATIONS, DOCUMENTATION, & RESEARCH.

152

OBJECT DOCUMENTATION LOG

Object:

Dimensions:

Material:

Inventory Date:

Location Found:

Visual Description/sketches:

Potential Categories:

Additional Notes:

Fieldworker's Initials:

153

154

EXPERIENCE DOCUMENTATION LOG

Date:

Time:

Location:

Subject/Event:

Visual Description/sketches, colors, textures, smells, shapes, materials:

Additional Notes:

Fieldworker's Initials:

155

156

OBJECT DOCUMENTATION LOG

Object:

Dimensions:

Material:

Inventory Date:

Location Found:

Visual Description/sketches:

Potential Categories:

Additional Notes:

Fieldworker's Initials:

158

EXPERIENCE DOCUMENTATION LOG

Date:

Time:

Location:

Subject/Event:

Visual Description/sketches, colors, textures, smells, shapes, materials:

Additional Notes:

Fieldworker's Initials:

159

160

OBJECT DOCUMENTATION LOG

Object:

Dimensions:

Material:

Inventory Date:

Location Found:

Visual Description/sketches:

Potential Categories:

Additional Notes:

Fieldworker's Initials:

162

EXPERIENCE
DOCUMENTATION LOG

Date:

Time:

Location:

Subject/Event:

Visual Description/sketches, colors, textures, smells, shapes, materials:

Additional Notes:

Fieldworker's Initials:

RESEARCH NOTES
(CONNECT THE DOTS)

165

166

MAKE A STORAGE POCKET

1. CUT OUT SLIT AS MARKED.

2. TAPE THIS PAGE TO THE NEXT ONE ALONG THREE SIDES.

TAPE

3. PLACE FLAT ITEMS INSIDE.

CUT OUT

TAPE HERE →

169

A PLACE TO GLUE FOUND OBJECTS.

EXPERIENCE COLLECTION

DATE	DESCRIPTION	LOCATION

EXPERIENCE COLLECTION

DATE	DESCRIPTION	LOCATION

OVERHEARD CONVERSATIONS

RESEARCH NOTES
(CONNECT THE DOTS)

LIST PAGES

COLORS

SMELLS

SOUNDS

_____
_____
_____
_____
_____
_____
_____
_____
_____
_____
_____
_____
_____

TASTES   TEXTURES

_____   _____

_____   _____

_____   _____

_____   _____

_____   _____

_____   _____

_____   _____

_____   _____

_____   _____

_____   _____

_____   _____

_____   _____

_____   _____

_____   _____

EXPERIENCE COLLECTION

DATE	DESCRIPTION	LOCATION

EXPERIENCE COLLECTION

DATE	DESCRIPTION	LOCATION

OBJECT TAGS
(FOR DOCUMENTING YOUR COLLECTIONS, CLUES, & EVIDENCE.) ATTACH USING STRING.

OBJECT:
DATE:
O LOCATION:
DESCRIPTION:

OBJECT:
DATE:
O LOCATION:
DESCRIPTION:

OBJECT:
DATE:
O LOCATION:
DESCRIPTION:

OBJECT:
DATE:
O LOCATION:
DESCRIPTION:

OBJECT:
DATE:
O LOCATION:
DESCRIPTION:

OBJECT:
DATE:
O LOCATION:
DESCRIPTION:

OBJECT:
DATE:
O LOCATION:
DESCRIPTION:

OBJECT:
DATE:
O LOCATION:
DESCRIPTION:

OBJECT:
DATE:
O LOCATION:
DESCRIPTION:

OBJECT:
O DATE:
LOCATION:
DESCRIPTION:

184

185

LIST PAGES

COLORS

SMELLS

SOUNDS

TASTES

TEXTURES

_____
_____
_____
_____
_____
_____
_____
_____
_____
_____
_____
_____
_____

_____
_____
_____
_____
_____
_____
_____
_____
_____
_____
_____
_____
_____

EXPERIENCE COLLECTION

DATE	DESCRIPTION	LOCATION

EXPERIENCE COLLECTION

DATE	DESCRIPTION	LOCATION

190

191

SETTING UP A SHOWING FOR YOUR MUSEUM

CHOOSING A SPACE

AN ART OR MUSEUM SHOW DOES NOT HAVE TO BE IN A GALLERY SETTING TO BE VALID. ONE OF THE MOST INVENTIVE SHOWS I HAVE EVER EXPERIENCED WAS A WOMAN WHO CREATED HER OWN GALLERY OUT OF THE BACK OF AN OLD TRUCK IN AMSTERDAM. SHE WOULD DRIVE IT AROUND TO VARIOUS LOCATIONS AND CHARGE A SMALL ADMISSION TO HELP PAY FOR GAS. I LOVED THE IDEA THAT A GALLERY COULD BE WHEREVER AND WHATEVER YOU WANT. THERE ARE NO RULES. ON A SIDEWALK, IN YOUR BACKYARD, IN A TREE, IN YOUR GARAGE, IN THIS BOOK, IN A SUITCASE, OUT OF THE BACK OF YOUR CAR. ALL YOU NEED IS A SIGN TELLING PEOPLE WHAT YOU ARE DOING, A FEW LABELS, AND AN INVITATION OF SOME KIND.

DISPLAY METHODS

TRY TO COME UP WITH SOME DIFFERENT WAYS OF DISPLAYING YOUR COLLECTIONS.

SOME IDEAS:

HANGING THINGS FROM THE CEILING (OR FROM TREE BRANCHES), LAYERING, FLOATING THINGS IN WATER. MAKING INTERESTING PATTERNS ON THE FLOOR, PUTTING THE OBJECTS IN HIDDEN PLACES AND MAKING A MAP FOR THEM, USING PUBLIC SPACES, FENCES, CLOTHING, PORTABLE SPACES, ETC.

IT HELPS TO MAKE LABELS FOR YOUR SHOW.

```
┌ ─ ─ ─ ─ ─ ─ ─ ─ ─ ─ ─ ─ ─ ─ ┐
│                              │
│   TITLE:                     │
│   MATERIAL:                  │
│   DATE:                      │
│   DESCRIPTION:               │
│                              │
│                              │
└ ─ ─ ─ ─ ─ ─ ─ ─ ─ ─ ─ ─ ─ ─ ┘
```

SOMETHING LIKE THIS

FILL IN THE BLANKS

ANOTHER OPTION IS TO USE A CODING SYSTEM (COLORED DOTS OR SOME KIND OF GRAPHIC), SO THAT VIEWERS HAVE TO ACTIVELY SEEK OUT THE TITLE AND EXPLANATION OF THE OBJECT THEMSELVES (LOCATED SOMEWHERE CLOSE BY). THIS METHOD INVOLVES THE VIEWERS IN THEIR OWN PROCESS AND EXPERIENCE OF EXPLORATION.

SENDING OUT INVITATIONS

CREATE A POSTER OR INVITATIONS THAT SOMEHOW REFLECT THE NATURE OR CONTENT OF THE SHOW. IDEAS: IF YOU HAVE SMALL THINGS, MAKE THE INVITES REALLY TINY. YOU COULD ALSO WRITE INVITATIONS ON OBJECTS THEMSELVES, SUCH AS LEAVES OR FOUND PAPER.

IDEAS TO MAKE YOUR SHOW INTERESTING

- TRY HOLDING YOUR VIEWING IN A SECRET LOCATION, WITH SOME KIND OF PUZZLE VIEWERS HAVE TO FIGURE OUT.
- GIVE OUT "MYSTERY BAGS"; PAPER LUNCH BAGS CONTAINING A FOUND OBJECT.
- SUPPLY FOOD AND DRINKS.
- IF YOUR FOCUS IS TACTILE WORK, YOU COULD HAND OUT BLINDFOLDS.
- CONSIDER DIFFERENT WAYS OF VIEWING THE SHOW, LIKE FROM DIFFERENT VANTAGE POINTS (UP HIGH AND LOW TO THE GROUND)
- WHAT ABOUT A MUSEUM THAT YOU MAIL TO PEOPLE?
- CREATE AN INTERACTIVE PIECE SUCH AS A SCAVENGER HUNT.

GLOSSARY

AMATEUR
1784: "ONE WHO HAS A TASTE FOR (SOMETHING)," FROM FR. AMATEUR "LOVER OF," FROM O. FR. FROM L. AMATOREM (NOM. AMATOR) "LOVER," FROM AMATUS PP. OF AMARE "TO LOVE"   SOURCE: WIKIPEDIA

*AUTHOR'S NOTE: THE ACTIVITIES IN THIS BOOK INVOLVE SEEING THE WORLD FROM THE PERSPECTIVE OF AN AMATEUR, ONE WHO DOES SOMETHING SOLELY FOR THE LOVE OF IT WITHOUT ATTACHMENT TO OUTCOME.

ART
ONE SENSE OF THE WORD "ART" IS CLOSE TO THE OLDER LATIN MEANING, WHICH ROUGHLY TRANSLATES TO "SKILL" OR "CRAFT", AND ALSO FROM AN INDO-EUROPEAN ROOT MEANING "ARRANGEMENT" OR "TO ARRANGE." IN THIS SENSE, ART IS WHATEVER IS DESCRIBED AS HAVING UNDERGONE A DELIBERATE PROCESS OF ARRANGEMENT BY AN AGENT. SOURCE: WIKIPEDIA

EAR CLEANING
A SYSTEMATIC PROGRAM FOR TRAINING THE EARS TO LISTEN MORE DISCRIMINATINGLY TO SOUNDS, PARTICULARLY THOSE OF THE ENVIRONMENT. SOURCE: THE SOUNDSCAPE, BY R. MURRAY SCHAFER

ETHNOGRAPHY
THE DOCUMENTATION AND ANALYSIS OF EVERYDAY LIFE AND PRACTICE OF A PARTICULAR CULTURE THROUGH FIELD RESEARCH.

EVERYDAY TOURISM
ALWAYS SEEING THE WORLD WITH NEW EYES.

FIELD STUDY
THE PRACTICE OF CONDUCTING RESEARCH ON A VARIETY OF SUBJECTS IN THEIR NATURAL ENVIRONMENT OR HABITAT.

FOUND OBJECT
AN OBJECT THAT IS PRE-EXISTING (NOT CREATED) AND ORIGINALLY INTENDED FOR A DIFFERENT PURPOSE. IT CAN BE MASS PRODUCED

198

OR FROM NATURE. THESE OBJECTS ARE OFTEN FOUND IN THE MIDST OF EVERYDAY LIFE AND PLACED IN A NEW CONTEXT FOR ARTISTIC PURPOSES.

GLEANING

IN THE TRADITIONAL SENSE, GLEANING WAS DONE BY PEASANTS WHO COLLECTED WHAT WAS LEFT IN THE FIELDS AFTER THE HARVEST. IN THE CONTEMPORARY SENSE, GLEANING REFERS TO THE PRACTICE OF SCAVENGING YOUR COMMUNITY FOR ITEMS THAT HAVE BEEN DISCARDED BY OTHERS, SOMETIMES FOOD, OBJECTS, HOUSE-HOLD GOODS, OR RECYCLED MATERIALS.

INDETERMINATE

SOMETHING THAT IS NOT KNOWN EXACTLY, OR WITHOUT A PREDICTABLE RESULT OR OUTCOME.

QUOTIDIAN

ORDINARY OR EVERYDAY, ESPECIALLY WHEN MUNDANE. SOURCE: OXFORD AMERICAN DICTIONARY

READY-MADE

THE TERM "READY-MADE" WAS USED BY THE FRENCH ARTIST MARCEL DUCHAMP IN THE EARLY 1900s TO REFER TO MANUFACTURED (MASS-PRODUCED) OBJECTS, AS USED IN THE CONTEXT OF ART (AS OPPOSED TO THEIR ORIGINAL INTENT). DUCHAMP OFTEN USED READY-MADE ITEMS IN HIS WORK. THESE PIECES BEGAN A DIALOGUE ABOUT WHAT ART IS AND WHO DETERMINES WHAT ART IS. SOURCE: THE TATE COLLECTION GLOSSARY, EXCERPT FROM THE MAY 1917 ISSUE OF THE AVANT-GARDE MAGAZINE THE BLIND MAN

SCIENCE

THE INTELLECTUAL AND PRACTICAL ACTIVITY ENCOMPASSING THE SYSTEMATIC STUDY OF STRUCTURE AND BEHAVIOR OF THE PHYSICAL AND NATURAL WORLD THROUGH OBSERVATION AND EXPERIMENT. SOURCE: OXFORD AMERICAN DICTIONARY

BIBLIOGRAPHY

ABRAM, D. THE SPELL OF THE SENSUOUS: PERCEPTION AND LANGUAGE IN A MORE-THAN-HUMAN WORLD. NEW YORK, PANTHEON BOOKS: 1996.

BACHELARD, G., AND M. JOLAS. THE POETICS OF SPACE. BOSTON, BEACON PRESS: 1994.

BUCHANAN-SMITH, P.G. SPECK: A CURIOUS COLLECTION OF UNCOMMON THINGS. NEW YORK, PRINCETON ARCHITECTURAL PRESS: 2001.

CALVINO, I. IF ON A WINTER'S NIGHT A TRAVELER. NEW YORK, HARCOURT BRACE JOVANOVICH: 1981.

CLASSEN, C. WORLDS OF SENSE: EXPLORING THE SENSES IN HISTORY AND ACROSS CULTURES. LONDON, ROUTLEDGE: 1993.

DOLPHIN, L., ED. EVIDENCE: THE ART OF CANDY JERNIGAN. SAN FRANCISCO, CHRONICLE BOOKS: 1999.

FELD, S. SOUND AND SENTIMENT: BIRDS, WEEPING, POETICS, AND SONG IN KALULI EXPRESSION. PHILADELPHIA, UNIVERSITY OF PENNSYLVANIA PRESS: 1990.

FER, B. THE INFINITE LINE: RE-MAKING ART AFTER MODERNISM. NEW HAVEN, CONN. YALE UNIVERSITY PRESS: 2004.

FLETCHER, A. THE ART OF LOOKING SIDEWAYS. LONDON, PHAIDON: 2001.

FULLER, R.B., ET AL. I SEEM TO BE A VERB. NEW YORK, BANTAM BOOKS: 1970.

GABLIK, S. THE REENCHANTMENT OF ART. NEW YORK, THAMES AND HUDSON: 2002.

HANH, THICH NHAT. PEACE IS EVERY STEP: THE PATH OF MINDFULNESS IN EVERYDAY LIFE. NEW YORK, BANTAM: 1991.

HEMENWAY, T. GAIA'S GARDEN: A GUIDE TO HOME-SCALE PERMACULTURE. WHITE RIVER JUNCTION, VT., CHELSEA GREEN PUB. CO.: 2001.

HESSE, H. WANDERING: NOTES AND SKETCHES. NEW YORK, FARRAR, STRAUS & GIROUX: 1972.

HIGHMORE, B. THE EVERYDAY LIFE READER, LONDON, ROUTLEDGE: 2002.

JAMES, W. THE VARIETIES OF RELIGIOUS EXPERIENCE. CIRENCESTER, UK, COLLECTOR'S LIBRARY: 2006.

KENT, C., AND J. STEWARD. LEARNING BY HEART: TEACHINGS TO FREE THE CREATIVE SPIRIT. NEW YORK, BANTAM: 1992.

KENT, M.C., HARVEY COX, AND SAMUEL A. EISENSTEIN. SISTER CORITA. PHILADELPHIA, PILGRIM PRESS: 1968.

KIRKHAM, P. CHARLES AND RAY EAMES: DESIGNERS OF THE TWENTIETH CENTURY. CAMBRIDGE, MASS., MIT PRESS: 1995.

KNECHTEL, J. TRASH. CAMBRIDGE, MASS., MIT PRESS: 2007.

KRAUSSE, J., AND C. LICHTENSTEIN, EDS. YOUR PRIVATE SKY: R. BUCKMINSTER FULLER, THE ART OF DESIGN SCIENCE. LARS MÜLLER, BADEN: 1999.

MAU, B., ET AL. MASSIVE CHANGE. LONDON, PHAIDON: 2004.

MUNARI, B. DESIGN AS ART. HARMONDSWORTH, UK, PENGUIN: 1971.

NEW, J. DRAWING FROM LIFE: THE JOURNAL AS ART. NEW YORK, PRINCETON ARCHITECTURAL PRESS: 2005.

OLIVEROS, P. DEEP LISTENING: A COMPOSER'S SOUND PRACTICE. iUNIVERSE, 2005.

PEREC, G. LIFE, A USER'S MANUAL. BOSTON, D.R. GODINE: 1978.

PEREC, G., AND J. STURROCK. SPECIES OF SPACES AND OTHER PIECES. LONDON, PENGUIN: 1997.

ROBBINS, T. SKINNY LEGS AND ALL. NEW YORK, BANTAM: 1990.

SABINI, M., ED. THE EARTH HAS A SOUL: THE NATURE WRITINGS OF C.G. JUNG. BERKELEY, CALIF., NORTH ATLANTIC BOOKS: 2002.

SCHWARTZ, I., AND E. ANNINK, EDS. BRIGHT MINDS, BEAUTIFUL IDEAS: PARALLEL THOUGHTS IN DIFFERENT TIMES: BRUNO MUNARI, CHARLES AND RAE EAMES, MARTÍ GUIXÉ, AND JURGEN BEY. AMSTERDAM, BIS PUBLISHERS: 2003.

SHERINGHAM, M. EVERYDAY LIFE: THEORIES AND PRACTICES FROM SURREALISM TO THE PRESENT. OXFORD, OXFORD UNIVERSITY PRESS: 2006.

SNYDER, G. (2007) "WRITERS AND THE WAR AGAINST NATURE," SHAMBHALA SUN 16:40.

SOLNIT, R. A FIELD GUIDE TO GETTING LOST. NEW YORK, VIKING: 2005.

TAYLOR, D.A. DOCUMENTING MARITIME FOLKLIFE: AN INTRODUCTORY GUIDE. WASHINGTON, DC, LIBRARY OF CONGRESS: 1992.

ZORN, J., ED. ARCANA II: MUSICIANS ON MUSIC. NEW YORK, HIPS ROAD: 2007.

ALL BOOKS
CONTINUE IN
THE BEYOND...

—ITALO CALVINO

THIS BOOK IS DEDICATED TO TILDEN SMITH PITCHER, WHO WAS BORN DURING THE COMPLETION OF THIS BOOK. YOU HAVE SO MANY WONDERFUL ADVENTURES AHEAD OF YOU.

THANK YOU TO:
JEFFERSON PITCHER (MY PARTNER IN EXPLORATION AND LIFE), MY AGENT FAITH HAMLIN, MY EDITOR MEG LEDER, AND PUBLISHER JOHN DUFF (WHOSE TRUST IN MY VISION ENCOURAGES ME TO GO FURTHER), TOMIE HAHN MY ETHNOGRAPHY EXPERT, FLUXUS, AND ALL OF MY FAVORITE TEACHERS WHO PUT ME ON THE PATH OF EXPLORATION: DR. BRYANT E. GRIFFITH, ROSS MENDES, LINDA MONTGOMERY, SHIRLEY YANOVER, PAULINE OLIVEROS, GEORGE WALKER.
AND TO ALL MY FAMILY AND FRIENDS NEAR AND FAR.

THE AUTHOR INCOGNITO

KERI SMITH IS THE AUTHOR OF SEVERAL BOOKS INCLUDING WRECK THIS JOURNAL: AN INVITATION TO EXPLORE 'CREATIVE DESTRUCTION'. READ MORE AT WWW.KERISMITH.COM

NOTE: THE PHOTOS ON PAGES 6, 18, 26, 39, 54, 72, 74, 98, 124, 126, 133, 144, 151, 193, AND 195 WERE TAKEN BY JEFFERSON PITCHER IN VARIOUS PLACES IN SPAIN, MOROCCO, AND TROY, N.Y. THE REST WERE TAKEN BY THE AUTHOR.